TACKLE  & TACTICS

Ken Townley

Published by
Paisley-Wilde Publishing Ltd
1 Grosvenor Square, Sheffield S2 4MS

First published in 1991 by
Paisley-Wilde Publishing Ltd.
1 Grosvenor Square,
Sheffield S2 4MS

© Ken Townley

British Library Cataloguing in Publication Data

Ken Townley
Tackle and Tactics
1. Carp Angling
1 Title
799. 1'752

ISBN 1 871700 15 9

Produced, Typeset and Published by
Paisley-Wilde Publishing Ltd.

Printed by
Gibbons Barford Print Ltd.

CONTENTS

The author in typical pose. Ken is a prolific catcher of big carp.

INTRODUCTION

I suppose the modern carp fishing scene must appear rather confusing to the newcomer or the outsider. So much jargon and technical mumbo-jumbo. You only have to look in the weekly angling press to read something like... "Caught on a lead cored helicopter rig with a size six Piggyback and 15lb Silkworm. 12lbs b.s. super abrasive resistant line, was used on a 4500 Aero G.T. Baitrunner, the rod a 13 foot woven Kevlar/high Modulus fibre carbon filament, wound in 3k carbon fibres of 3lbs test curve throwing a 4 ounce lead."

You what???

So I hope this section of the book may help dispel the clouds a little and sort out the hype from reality. I suppose it is aimed really at the young and at newcomers to carp fishing, for by now most experienced anglers have their own ideas about the gear they need. Having said which we can all learn from the thoughts and experiences of others, so hopefully there is something in here for everyone.

Carp fishing is a boom industry, of that there is no doubt, yet as recently as the mid seventies there were hardly any specialist tackle dealers around. Most items of carp fishing tackle were home made, or conversions of existing, rather unsatisfactory items. Nowadays, I'd guess that most tackle dealers carry at least 25% of their total stock in the form of specialist tackle.

Just look at the number of books and magazines around these days. That will show you just how much the market has grown. Again, going back a couple of decades, there was a dearth of decent reading matter for carp anglers. Of course there were the books and articles of Fred J. Taylor and Richard Walker; the Jack Hilton classic "Quest for Carp", and the magazine contributions of Jim Gibbinson, George Sharman, Terry Eustace, and a young Rod Hutchinson. We have the now defunct magazine "Angling" to thank for introducing carp fishing to a wider readership, coincidentally offering the first opportunity to write about the subject to some of today's most respected carp anglers. Their articles were devoured and dissected for every scrap of available information.

I have been around carp fishing a long time now (some would say too long!) and I have grown up with the new developments, watched as carp fishing became "mortal" if you like. Thanks to new tackle and bait developments carp started becoming easier to catch. In consequence the fish began to get wise and ever more sophisticated tackle was introduced to try and get under their guard. Today the market place is jammed with gizzmos and gimmicks all surrounded by a mountain of hype. Be warned that a sense of perspective is essential when you are about to part with your hard earned cash. For instance, what might be a mighty power casting rod in one man's hands, may be a totally unsuitable flop in another.

Take a look at the types of waters you are likely to be fishing most. You will need to match the tackle you buy to the waters you fish. Small intimate waters call for delicate presentation, while the big 100 acre pits will require more substantial tackle to get out to where the lunkers live. If you fish a wide variety of waters, you may want to own separate rod/reel combinations for each type. This is expensive I know, but a look in the second hand Swap Shop in Angler's Mail often yields a few bargains.

Before I go on to examine the market in detail, can I just make a couple of points? First off, it will be impossible to cover the tackle section without mentioning a number of trade names. So let me make it clear that I have no personal or commercial involvement with any of the companies named. If, say the name Gardner, Hutchinson or Nash crops up quite a lot, it is simply because they make good products and offer a wide range. When I mention rods and reels by name it isn't advertising…I haven't been got at by publicity seeking manufacturers. It is natural that I may tend to lean favourably towards the manufacturers of the tackle I use myself, but I hope that doesn't mean I am not being objective about the subject. Where I don't like a product, I'll say so, but at the end of the day it is the individual buyer who has to choose. All I hope to do is guide.

The best way to examine the various ranges is by attending the shows and conferences arranged on a regional and national basis by The Carp Society, The National Association of Specialist Anglers (NASA) and the Carp Angler's Association. Here you can browse to your heart's content making sure that you choose tackle that is right for you at a price you can afford.

Finally you should think seriously about getting your tackle insured. It's my experience of life that things you think are never going to happen to you, invariably do! Look proudly out of the bivvy door at the gleaming stainless bankside gear. The big net, three rods and reels and three of the latest Optonics. Can you YOU afford to replace them if they're nicked from the bank or from your car? There's well over a thousand quid's worth there staring you in the face. Either add your tackle to an existing household policy or take out separate cover. One day you'll be thankful that you did.

Ken Townley

Chris Yates... "...after all, look at the way Yatesy fishes!"

TACKLE

Right. Where to start? I hope this section will be able to cover the whole modern scene adequately. Inevitably there may be things that I miss out but it should cover all the fishing tackle that the present day carp angler will need. That's not to say that it will be a definitive list, and some may take exception that it is either too long or too short. Others may question if a particular item of tackle is indeed necessary in the first place. (After all. Look at the way Yatesy fishes!) The shopping list can be quite extensive, yet it need not break the bank. On the other hand, by the time you have really got the bug and carp fishing stops being a hobby and becomes a way of life, you'll find good reasons (to you anyway) for adding to the ever-growing mountain of gear that gets dragged along each trip.

"...the ever growing mountain of gear..."

RODS

Before you even think about choosing a new rod, remember that most rods are a compromise of one sort or another. Despite the claims of the tackle shops and the blank manufacturers, there is NO rod that will cast a three ounce lead to the horizon one minute, and then be perfectly suited to freelining in the margins the next. So take heed here, for there is a big bad misleading world of hype out there awaiting the unwary rod buyer.

There is also a whole new language to learn. Test curves, and taper designations just for starters. Don't get confused though. All you need know is that the higher the test curve, the stronger the rod. However, test curves give no indication of the action of the rod, so you'll need to know the difference between say a fast taper design and a slow taper one. There is also a rather hazy rule of thumb that says that the rod should cast approximately one ounce of weight for each pound of its test curve. To be honest I don't really know now valid this is, but I must say, it appears to hold water in most cases. Be warned though that it is a very rough guide and should not always be taken too literally.

A rod's action is important. The stiffer the rod (fast taper rods) the better the casting tool it becomes, while at the same time becoming a less perfect fish playing rod. Soft rods (slow taper rods) on the other hand are better for playing out fish, but cannot measure up to the casting abilities usually associated with fast taper, stiff rods.

I'd also like to remind all carp anglers that their rods don't HAVE to be made of the latest mega-tech, space age materials. People were catching carp on cane and fibre glass rods for years before carbon and Kevlar made their appearance. Even though they might seem unfashionable in this day and age, they have a lot going for them.

Fibre glass in particular is cheap, light, will cast a long way and has plenty of 'feel' when playing fish. Terry Eustace still sells the amazingly popular T24 Carp Rod, an 11.5 foot fibre glass rod that will handle most angling situations apart from truly long range, while North Western's SS5 is the perfect rod for snag fishing. It's action is so soft that it bends right through to the handle section, so in hook and hold situations, the rod does all the work, absorbing each desperate lunge without having to yield line.

I suppose that if you got a crowded room full of carp men all talking about carp rods, you'd be hard pushed to find two that see eye to eye, and I have to admit that there are now so many first rate carp rods on the market, that choosing the right tool for the job is getting ever more difficult. So before you buy you must look at the choice available to you with extreme caution, and I guess, a fair amount of scepticism. Many of the extravagant claims of the rod manufacturers can be taken with a pinch or two of salt. However, with a little bit of thought you will certainly be able to find a rod to suit you.

It goes without saying that, as with many aspects of carp tackle, there are horses for courses governing choice of rod and I think it is best that we divide the market up into three sections, covering three very different styles of fishing. Namely long range, by which I mean from in excess of 100 yards; medium range, which is from say 30-100 yards, and finally short range which is anything from the margins outwards. In fact, you'll often be able to use you medium range rods for margin fishing.

LONG RANGE

There is a section dealing with the specifications of long range carp fishing later on in the book, but for now can I just deal with the choice of rod for distance work. The most important thing to remember when buying a long range fishing rod, is to get one that you can handle physically. Now I suppose you're thinking that seems a stupidly obvious thing to say, but believe me, some of the truly specialised long range rods are high-tech thoroughbreds that need practice and a highly tuned casting style to get them to work at their best.

Fast taper rods such as the Horizon range, which are built on Century Composites blanks (also sold as the Express Range by some rod builders) have strong, very stiff butt sections, with the major part of their action in the top 4-5 feet. These are among the best distance casting rods on the market at the moment, but like many very fast tapered designs they are not everybody's cup of tea. The stiff butt section leaves all the fish playing properties of the rod concentrated in the top third of the rod. If you're not used to this tippy action, this stiffness can have dire consequences when playing hard fighting fish in close under the tip. Hook pulls or even line breaks can catch out the unwary if you aren't used to handling fish on stiff, fast taper rods. On the other hand, if you want to cast long distances you have to make some sacrifices in action and 'feel'.

I have absolutely no doubt whatsoever in my mind that fast taper designs are the best ones for long distance casting, and I use Horizons myself. Over the years I have grown used to their limitations under the tip, and even though I always use barbless hooks, I don't believe that I lose fish under the tip that I would otherwise land on softer compound rods. I think that now, after four seasons with the rods, I am casting better than I have ever done before, but it's taken quite a time for me to get the best out of these beasties. Yet I think this could be true for all fast taper rods. They can take a lot of getting used to, and the Horizons in particular are no respecters of a timid approach, so practise really does make perfect.

There really is a very wide choice open to the distance caster so it pays to take your time and canvass other opinions before making any decisions. All the top manufacturers now offer meaty 13 footers capable of throwing four once leads a long way. I suppose the new Hutchinson 3.5lb test and the North Western Dyneema 2.75lb fast taper rods probably compete for the title of the Rolls Royce of the distance casting world. Both are 13 feet long, beautifully made and a dream to handle. They are by no means cheap, but perfectly balanced casting machines never are.

There are some long distance rods on the market that make extraordinary claims for themselves, while at the same time stating that they are soft enough to use under the tip, which I must admit, I find hard to swallow, but I am assured that this is the case. Perhaps the most powerful of these is the Armalite 4lb test 13 footer. Certainly the whole Armalite range is very popular, but from a personal standpoint I have to say that I find them heavy and quite ponderous casting rods. That said, I have to admit that I have seen some very impressive casters using them to put baits out to 140 yards plus. On the other hand I have also watched many anglers struggle with the 13 foot 3lbs test curve rods which have become very popular over the past couple of seasons. In my article "Horizon Bashing" in Big Fish World 2 I stressed the importance of matching body weight, size and strength to the choice of specialist distance casting rod. For example, it is no good going for say the 13 foot 3lb Armalite if you are 5'5" tall and weigh 8 stone. You almost certainly won't be able to get the rod wound up enough to improve your distance. Remember, in distance casting tip speed is everything, and unless you can work the blank to its full potential you will loose out on tip speed and thus distance. You'd probably be far better off with a lighter 12 foot long rod such as the Catchum Sabre 2.25lb, or even the fast taper original Simpsons K.M. 1, which is an 11 foot model that still has plenty to recommend it, even after ten years on the market.

On the other hand, I've seen some mighty meaty lads who can use their strength properly to make the most of the power a rod like the Armalite, and I've seen casts that would take your breath away.

At the end of the day, I don't think it is any coincidence that the top rated professional surf casters use fast tape, rods, if for no other reason than they can get better tip speed, and I am convinced that the carp angler, looking for true long distance work MUST choose fast taper designs. Rod length is also important in distance work... but only up to a point. There are some 15 foot long rods on the market these days, and in theory the longer the rod, the greater the leverage (power?) and thus the greater the distance. This is fine, as far as it goes, but have you ever tried playing a fish on a fifteen foot rod? I have and it's painful. The strain on the wrist is enormous... twice that of a twelve footer. Remember to make allowances for your body weight/strength when deciding on rod length.

Finally can I just incur the wrath of rod builders everywhere and state quite categorically that I do not believe that silicone carbide rings make a ha'pth of difference to the casting properties of a rod for 99% of the anglers who fall for these expensive gimmicks.

Medium Range

Life gets a lot easier from now on in. The choice of pleasant, short to medium range rods is large, and most of them offer excellent fish playing qualities. Your main criteria should be price and finish. I would always suggest that you buy the best you can afford purely and simply because you are unlikely to chop and change your short to medium rods as often as you would a distance rod. I say this because I have seen anglers who should know better continually searching for ultimate distance from each new super-duper rod to come onto the market. With the shorter range rods, distance isn't the object.

So what do you look for in a medium range rod? Well I'd suggest a length of 12 feet and test curves of between 1.75 and 2.25lbs. The action should be fairly light but with plenty of strength in the butt section for maximum control under the tip. They can be of either fast or compound taper, for at these sort of distances the design isn't really a factor. Simply choose a rod that you feel happy with, at a price you can afford.

My wife Carole and I have been using a pair of Simpsons KM2 duel taper 12 foot, 1.75lbs test curve rods for about 6 years now and I cannot fault them. The action is sweet and sure with a lovely progressive through action that comes more and more into play as the fight nears the bank. Under the tip they play fish like a dream, yet I can still cast in excess of 80 yards with them using a 2 ounce bomb.

We also use a set of three of Hutchie's original Spirolite Mk. 2 12 footers. These have a slightly higher test curve of 2lbs and will cast slightly further than the Simpson rods. In fact the two rods are well matched for "feel" and playing qualities and I wouldn't want to part with either. Carole and I use these two sets for about 90% of our fishing, and I'm quite happy using them for margin work as well.

It is in this section of the market that we find the what I would call, the production line rods such as those from Shimano, Daiwa, Sundridge Tackle, Shakespeare and others. I have no experience of actually playing fish on any of these rods, but have seen them and waved them about in tackle shops… not the best way of getting the feel of a rod I know! I must say that I was impressed with the Daiwa and Shimano rods, but they always seem to me to appear lighter, less robust than their claimed test curves would suggest.

The new range from D.A.M. Tackle called the Andy Little Carp Rods look to be good value for money, well finished with a nice progressive action and my initial impressions have been very favourable. Of the factory built rods these seem to offer the best value for money. Certainly many of the others are not cheap.

Personally I think I'd prefer to have the blanks themselves professionally built by one of the excellent, top class rod builders and I'd be hard pushed to choose between any of the softer blanks from Tricast, Armalite, Sportex, North Western or the Conoflex range.

If you are choosing on a budget, many of the tackle shops offer some excellent value rods. The Bob Morris Carp/Specimen range, and The Tackle Box (Kent) range of less expensive rods, and Fosters Tackle of Birmingham offer quality rods at bargain prices; as do many other tackle shops throughout the country. Look around for the best bargains at the lower end of the price scale. Just because they are less expensive, doesn't necessarily mean that they are cheap and cheerful. Many of these rods at widely differing prices are built on the same blanks!

Finally, don't expect miracle distances from these rods. It is a mistake to think that by increasing the casting weight you automatically cast further. Rods in this bracket are designed for casting weights of around two ounces. By going up to say three, you are simply overloading the rod and slowing down the tips speed, which is what you need for distance work. If you want to cast further, come down a couple of pounds in the breaking strain of the line where this is feasible.

Short Range

From the margins out to about 30 yards, many of the rods in the proceeding category will cope quite happily with this sort of work. However, there is great delight in playing fish on delicate, soft little eleven footers of around 1.5lbs test curve, always providing that you are not taking too many risks with your chances of landing carp successfully. We have used a pair of sweet little carbon Sportex rods for almost ten years now and have just had them rebuilt by Bob Jones, and had the original twin legged Fuji rings replaced with single legged ones, thus softening the action even further. I originally bought them for Carole as they are very light in weight and thin in the butt: ideal for her small hands. With time though I have come to love them dearly. They are a dream to use with a wonderful action right through into the butt section.

A really silly-soft rod is the North Western SS5 which is a fibre blank. The action of this is described as "through" but I would suggest that "through and out the other side" would be a fairer description. I haven't tried it with mine, but I'm sure you could tie them in a knot! These rods are so soft that even the handle bends, but while they look and feel heavy and somewhat cumbersome, they are a delight to play fish on. Their ultra soft action also makes them a superb snag-fishing rod when matched with strong line. All the major blank manufacturers produce a range of soft, light rods that are ideal for margin fishing. I like the Tricast, North Western and Sportex carbon fibre ranges.

Rings, Grips and Reel Seats.

A good blank can be spoilt if poor quality fittings are used. The fixed reel seat itself should always be of of the screw locking type, preferably of lightweight carbon fibre. There is considerable argument between rod builders about the right and wrong way that these should be fitted. Bruce Ashby told me that he got so fed up arguing the toss with prospective customers that he now leaves the choice to them. My own preference is for the fixed end of the seat to be up the blank, for no other reason than I think it feels more comfortable this way. Also, if instead the screw section extends up towards the spigot, this can interfere with the fitting of a line clip.

As for the rod rings (also called guides). Well, I've already mentioned the silicon-carbide lined rod rings, but I like the single leg Fujis of the BSVLG pattern for my own rods. The twin leg Seymo flexi-seat guides are a fine alternative, and they don't alter the action or feel of the rod like some twin legged guides can.

Handles and the material in which they are finished are again really a matter for personal preference. I think cork looks and feels far nicer than Duplon or any of the other alternatives and I prefer full length handles of either material rather than abbreviated ones. (The latter have a tendency to slip out from under your arm while you are playing a fish!) I have seen a few rods spoilt by putting the reel fitting too close to the butt. Ask your rod builder for his advice as this distance can be critical and varies from blank to blank. Your personal casting style also needs to be taken into consideration. Overhead casters like the reel closer to the butt than across-the-chest ones. If you are tall or have long arms for your height, you will need a greater distance between the reel seat and the butt. Between 23-26" should suit all but the funniest shaped carp anglers.

Summary

Rods are probably the most expensive item of tackle you will buy so choose not only with care but also to suit your pocket. There are usually plenty of good second hand bargains to be found in the Anglers Mail Swap Shop pages: indeed I have bought most of my rods through the papers and am perfectly happy to admit it. I know many of you will be starting carp fishing on a shoestring so can I just give one final word of advice on the choice of rod.

If you are in any doubt about the type of rod to buy, I'd suggest going for one that will cope with distance work. You may start off fishing smallish waters, but even on five or six acre pools, the hot spot on the unfishable far bank may be over 100 yards away. The thing is that one day you are going to find yourself on a water where you can't reach the fish. This happened to me the first time I ever fished Savay when the Geoff Kemp 2lb rods I was using left me well short, and bottling up a top swim for someone else. You can always cast your long range rods shorter distances, but you cannot make a short or medium range rod cast further. Get my point?

Finally I have to say that I can't see ANY rod being worth two hundred pounds or more, but then I suppose if you want something badly enough you'll manage somehow!

Ken's wife Carole plays a fish under the tip on a compound taper rod.

REELS

Like rods, choosing a good carp fishing reel requires a bit of thought and consideration. Again there are a great many to choose from, and each have their advocates. I'm probably stating the obvious here, but as far as reels are concerned you really do get what you pay for. Quality costs money and there is no place for cheap, poor quality reels in the carp world.

I'd say that to all intents and purposes the fixed spool reel is the best suited to modern day carp fishing, though I can see a time coming when multipliers may be the true long distance casting reel in common use. Centre pins also have their place and I'll deal with them a little later on.

I use a wide variety of reels myself so first of all I'll just run through my choice and the reasons for choosing them.

For my distance work I am currently using Shimano Biomaster 4000 reels. They are simply a casting tool, with little in the way of gimmicky drags and whizz-kid clutches. They are compact and light, and have superb casting qualities, due to their 2-speed oscillation and cross line lay spool. This prevents the line bedding down upon itself during retrieve. The spool itself is long, wide and tapered and can hold a lot of line. I have a spare spool for each reel. For maximum distance I use six pound line with a fifteen pound shock leader, while the other spool holds fifteen pound line right through. The line lay of the Biomaster is so good that even with the fifteen on I can cast close to 100 yards with a three ounce lead on the Horizons, while the fine line I can cast in excess of 140 yards.

For medium range work I am still using the Abu 55s that I bought in the early 80s. It has become fashionable of late to knock these reels as old fashioned relics from the dark ages. That is nonsense. The 55s are splendid reels, and even though they are no longer made, they can be picked up through the second hand pages of the angling press. They aren't cheap, but they are quality reels and worth every penny. I have a whole box full of spare spools covering just about every eventuality, and I trust them enough to fish them off the clutch, Baitrunner style. The line lay isn't as good as the Shimanos but then I'm not after maximum distances, so it's not that important. The bale arm springs are tough, the bales themselves snap over well, and there is a roller bearing to keep line wear down.

On our light rods we are now using a pair of the little Shimano Carbomatic G.T.M.3000X reels. These were also bought for Carole to use, again for their lightness, but also for the shorter grip (reel stem) that is better suited to her hand size. This is something that is worth bearing in mind, for some reels look as if they've been designed with giants in mind. The clutch arrangement is 100% reliable and very progressive. It also incorporates a pre-set fighting drag that allows you to get into contact with a running fish quickly and without fuss. The spools hold enough 8 or 12 pound line for our needs, and while they don't have the line lay of the other Shimanos, or even the 55s, they are as sweet a little reel you could wish for. They weigh just 11 ounces yet are robust enough to give big fish plenty of wellie.

That's what I use, but there is a huge choice in the shops. No mention of reels would be complete without a mention of the famous Mitchell range. They seem to have been around since the dawn of time, and they are as good today as they ever were. The 300 and 410 were probably the top selling carp reels on the market for years, and they still hold favour with many top class anglers. I must also mention the-value-for-money range from Silstar, who have produced some excellent copies of certain well known Far Eastern products, with all the benefits of the high-tech reels at a lower price.

Of course, there are plenty of other manufacturers eager to have their share of the ever swelling carp fishing market. Browning's reels are well crafted and finished. Their rear drag system is smooth as silk and totally reliable. Ryobi too has a nice range to offer. With top carp man Andy Little now advising them, DAM Tackle are about to introduce their latest offering in the form of their revolutionary Quick CD Free Spool 350 offering. This much praised reel may well challenge the Shimano superiority once it becomes established and it certainly looks good, with Dam's usual high standard of engineering and finish.

Daiwa markets a fine selection of reels from budget priced, rear drag models, to top-of-the-range casting reels which are more than a match for the Biomaster. They have all the superb casting qualities you would expect from a tournament-casting reel, and a new tournament reel will soon be on the market that may well be the state of the art long distance reel that many of us have been waiting for. Mind you, at £150 a time, it'll have to be good!

Another one for the distance men is the Abu 57. Like the medium range 55 reel, this one is no longer manufactured... which I reckon is a crying shame. They were brilliant reels with good line lay and big spools and were very popular until the Shimanos and Daiwa casting reels hit the shops. Sadly Abu have failed to respond to the new challenges and I no longer feel they have carp fishing reels to match the competition.

No review of carp fishing reels would be complete without a mention of the Shimano Baitrunner series. Over the past few years this range has taken the market by storm, and I doubt I'd be far off the mark in saying that they are now the most popular reels currently available. The free spool Baitrunner facility was a reel breakthrough, allowing line to be taken off the reel while the

REELS FOR CARP FISHING

Shimano Aero GT 4500

Ryobi

Daiwa SS3000

.Centre Pin

Shimano

DAM Quick FS 350

bale arm is still closed. The Baitrunner tension is fully adjustable so that with rod lock tactics line can only be gained with considerable effort on the part of the fish. This is ideal for long range fishing tight to snags or weedbeds when line stretch is an important factor.

Now, with the introduction of the Aero GT Baitrunners, Shimano have added the Biomaster's long, tapered spool and the twin oscillating line lay system to the already popular Baitrunner series. Add to that an easily adjustable rear drag that seems utterly reliable and I think you can see why this range has become the market leader. There are several sizes within the range, the 4000 and 4500 being perhaps the best all round models for both distance and medium range work. Not cheap, but excellent quality and value. Mind you... I still prefer my Biomasters!

Finally, I cannot close this look at reels without mentioning centre pins. This will quickly earn plenty of Brownie Points from Chris Yates who has been using the 'pin' for much of his carp fishing for years. For margin and close range stalking they cannot be bettered, their great advantage over fixed spool reels being their direct 1:1 gearing. In other words you are in absolute control over every inch of line yielded to a fighting fish. There's not bale arm to worry about, no tension to adjust. You strike and are straight into the fish. The "feel" of a big carp fighting it out on a centre pin bears no comparison to the rather remote "feel" from a fixed spool. There aren't many good centre pins around these days and even second hand they command top prices. The Match Aerial, Rapidex and Trudex models are brilliant, while the Grice & Young centre pins such as the Royal Avon Supreme and the Matchmaker are robust, free-running and of high quality. If you've never tried centre pin carp fishing, give it a try. You don't know what you're missing.

That's got the important side of carp fishing sorted out. Put line on your reels and you're away. You can now go out and catch fish... in theory! If only it was that simple. Truth to tell, carp fishing has almost become too technical for its own good. It may well be the case that we have become to dependent on unnecessary gadgets and gimmickry to catch our fish, but for all that, somehow I can't see that great innovator Richard Walker turning in his grave just yet awhile.

BITE ALARMS

Chris Yates will tell you that bite alarms (buzzers) are noisy, intrusive and unnecessary and a total anathema to him. Certainly there are times when I could wring the neck of some thoughtless so and so who's forever adjusting and playing with his alarm… usually at maximum volume; but if you are going to fish long sessions then some form of audible alarm is vital. It just isn't physically possible to concentrate on the indicators for long periods without the buzzers there to take the strain. At night, or when you feel you must get some sleep the alarms are there to let you know you've got a run, and I don't care what you say… nobody can fish properly for more than about 12 hours without getting some sort of rest or relaxation. So bite alarms are almost as vital an item of tackle as rods and reels.

It seems strange to think that bite alarms have been around as long as they have. In fact I believe Dick Walker was the first to develop an electronic system for detecting takes way back at the time of the formation of the Carp Catchers Club. Even as recently as 1980 George Sharman published the full, complicated details of converting Walker's original antenna alarm idea to a full alarm system rather than the established buzzer and bulb set up. All this came just months before the now familiar Optonic indicators became generally available. Looking at the pictures in Sharman's classic "Carp and the Carp Angler" it seems strange to think that just about a decade ago there wasn't an Optonic to be seen on the bankside. Yet over the past ten years this alarm has become the number one choice for I'd guess about 90% of the carp anglers fishing today.

I'll cover the different types of systems briefly here. Though there are many models and designs available, the choice really falls between the two main systems. These are the antenna alarm such as the Delkim converted Herons or the AJS alarm on the one hand, and the wheel or roller alarm such as the Bitech Viper, the Optonic, the Sensitron or the Andy Little Roller Alarm.

The Optonic type of alarm feeds the line over a roller within the housing, at the end of which is a two or four blade beam breaking paddle. As the line passes over the roller the paddle is turned to interrupt a battery activated beam of light and switch on an audible alarm. Antenna alarms operate on a different system. Here the line is fed around an antenna. Any increase in the tension of the line asserts a pull against the antenna itself which in turn closes a pair of contacts which operate the alarm. Generally the wheel and roller designs are more expensive than the antenna systems, but they are also more complicated so there's more to go wrong with them!

Bitech
Viper

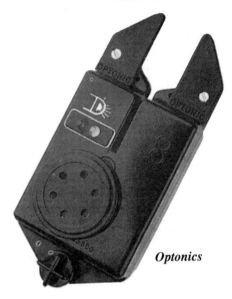

Optonics

BITE
ALARMS

Diawa
Sensitron

AJS Antenna Buzzer

Both kinds of bite alarm systems have their advantages and disadvantages. Certainly on some of the true pressure waters where the carp have become ultra shy of baits, and screaming runs are getting rarer, the antenna alarm does give a better indication that a bait has been picked up.

Let us imagine a wary fish has mouthed the bait, and the hook has the lightest of holds without penetrating properly. Instead of running (and thereby probably hooking itself) the carp remains almost motionless trying to get rid of the hook without pulling against the full weight of the bomb. This would result in a slight tightening of the line. The best you could hope for from an Optonic would be either a few erratic bleeps or maybe just a single one. In fact in some extreme cases you might not get any sign at all that a fish was on the other end. If this sounds a bit far fetched, let me assure you that it can and does happen, on more and more waters. Now while the roller design might let you down under these circumstances, the antenna system would register the extra tension on the line with a buzz, and this would be maintained as long as the line was subjected to the increased tension. Thus an effective strike could probably be made against such a shy biting fish, whereas you might be undecided whether to strike at a single bleep from an Optonic.

Of course there are ways around this even when using the wheel and roller alarms. The 12 blade beam breaking paddle now sold by Kevin Nash for Optonics goes a long way towards acquiring a more positive signal, and these combined with very heavy indicators should ensure that there is enough indication from the alarm to register sufficient warning of events at the business end.

One disadvantage of antenna systems is that they don't register drop back bites at all well, so if much of your fishing is done tight to far margins where drop backs are the order of the day, you should be aware of this bugbear.

All in all I have to say that the wheel and roller alarms are better for everyday carp fishing than the antenna systems. However, keep an open mind. As a rule antenna alarm systems are considerably cheaper and do a first class job.

I have heard lots of favourable whispers about the new Daiwa Sensitron Alarm, but at the time of writing no details have come through. But keep an eye out for this new high-tech buzzer in the new future.

Most modern alarms are waterproofed to a certain degree by the manufacturers, bit I'd rather be safe than sorry. I coat the two halves of the housing with a silicone sealant and spray the circuits with WD40 or similar. If I'm using extension leads, I also spray the silicone into the socket.

Talking of extension leads… Many of today's electronic buzzers are self contained. They have powerful speakers and volume and tone adjustments which means that they can be heard at the other end of the lake. There is NOTHING guaranteed to annoy most carp anglers more than getting out of bed in the middle of the night to hit what he thought was his own screaming buzzers, only to find it's some idiot with perfect hearing showing off miles away down the bank. I nearly always use extension leads and a remote sounder box with my Delkims. The only time I won't bother with them is when there is nobody else on the water with me, or on short sessions. Even then I have the volume turned low. Please, there is no need for ghetto blasting buzzers, and if taken to excess we could find ourselves with a total ban on audible alarms on some waters.

Designed for efficiency - and good to look at. A modern carp set up in use. The tackle includes Spirolite rods, Abu 55 reels, Gardner rod pod, Delkim buzzers, Gardner brass Optonic bolts and forks, Gardner banksticks and buzzer bars, Solar Tackle indicators and needles, Terry Eustace rear rod rests.

BIVVIES

I hate to think how many hours I've spent staring up at the green ceiling of a bivvy. I have been around long enough to remember the days of the Send Marketing canvas bivvies. They were heavy and cumbersome, they flapped in the wind and you had to crawl in and out of them like a bloody hunchback. But they were all we had, and at least they offered one considerable benefit that some modern bivvies don't… they were warm!

Things have come on a lot since then, though I believe Kevin Nash still makes canvas overwraps for the traditionalists. The trend for lightweight, easily erectable bivvies started in the late seventies/early eighties with Richie's Water Lot. This has now been developed into the storm sides or wrap-around idea, where the umbrella, itself forms part of the protection. They are light and convenient, as the sides can be stowed, still in position on the folded umbrella after a session and the whole thing can be put up or down in seconds. They have a slight disadvantage in that they can be a little restrictive inside, but from the numbers I see on the banks, they are certainly the number one choice for most carp men.

Next comes the overwrap bivvy. As the name suggests the umbrella is simply used as a solid frame over which the tailor-made bivvy is spread. I have used one of the superb Dave Barnes models for years now. Sadly now out of production, it has withstood some of the most horrendous weather, that has reduced other overwraps to tattered fragments, including the Oct. '87 and the Jan. '90 storms. The nearest I've seen to the old Barnes Aquashed has been the JEKK Shelters which look to be almost the same design. Of course the ubiquitous Kevin Nash also makes a series of bivvies including wraparounds, overcraps (sic) and his oval brolly system (which seems now to have cured it's teething troubles to become a first class and spacious bivvy). Bob Frost sells a nice range as well, including a rather trendy, yet very attractive 50" Camouflaged Bivvy made to Ministry of Defence specifications.

For the short session, dry weather angler the mini stormsides, like those offered by Bob Frost, have much to commend them. These are designed to protect the head and foot ends of your bedchair from the elements, and are simply velcroed onto the lower four panels of the standard brolly.

Though not so popular these days, the mushroom type bivvy still enjoys a limited following, particularly with long session couples who fish together. Carole and I have used one of the Dave Barnes 45" bivvies for the past seven years. Even though it is only a 45" it holds two bedchairs, all our luggage and tackle, plus food burner etc. It is truly a pity that real quality products like these are not made anymore.

Finally, there are the new bivvies that are really dome type tents. The E.T. Bivvy Dome was the first of these on the market and it quickly showed the versatility and convenience of this type of camp. The sewn-in groundsheet, the fly screen door and the fly sheet overwrap is what many of us have been waiting for. If it wasn't for the fact that I often fish with my missus and share a bivvy, I'd have no hesitation in getting the E.T. Dome. As it is I think it is a bit too small for two bedchairs and the rest of our parafinalia, so we have now bought the bigger Rod Hutchinson version. It is a smashing bivvy... I can't fault it. Plenty of room with a two-part zip-up door with an inner fly screen and an outer door. The canopy is a blessing in bad weather, while the sewn in groundsheet is tough and completely waterproof.

The latest dome tent on offer is Chris Manifold's Aqua Products' Bivi-Dome. This is a sort of buy as you go product with the base dome offered at around eighty pounds and then a series of add-on extras such as a storm porch, an inner tent and side vents at varying prices.

I certainly see these types of bivvy as showing the way ahead for today's long stay carp anglers. They are far lighter than any conventional bivvy arrangement that depends on an umbrella for its support. The only problem might arise in the minds of some of the more short sighted, anti-carp angling club committees who may see fit to ban "camping". Pathetic isn't it.

Before I leave the subject of bivvies, I must mention the umbrella type bivvies with the sides being an integral part of the tent. Both Steades and Fox International are now offering this type of bivvy and the Fox system in particular looks very promising, with three different set-ups all of which incorporate storm porches.

A word about bivvy pegs. Some of the silly looking things I've seen defy belief. The middle of a force 10 storm is no time to discover that your pegs are not robust enough, long enough or generally not man enough to secure your carp house. There are some well made stainless steel pegs on the market. Solar Tackle's are probably the best and will probably outlast anything else around. On the other hand there are some cheaper alternatives around if you just use your eyes. I use either roofing ties or concrete fencing post tie-bolts from all good builders merchants. These are very tough and all you'll need to adapt them to bivvy pegs is to put a point on them with an electrical grindstone. They are available in various lengths and I find the 10" versions are the best. They feature a fine threaded end which helps them bite in gravel or stony banks.

Finally, there are those who prefer to kip under no other protection than an umbrella a la Carp Fever. These guys have my full admiration. At my age that's too much for me, but several years back I too was one of these "hard buggers" who couldn't care less about the elements. There is really a very limited choice on the umbrella market. The massive Kevin Nash Oval brolly will cover you from head to toe, and of course the top selling Wavelock

Nubrollis from Steades are probably the most popular brollies on the market.

I suppose your choice will always depend on the amount of long session and winter fishing that you do. I have been very happy with my overwrap and mushroom bivvies but I think the Hutchinson Bivvy Tent will get a lot more outings now.

The Dave Barnes Mushroom Bivvy. Note the groundsheet for added warmth, and to keep out the damp.

BANKSIDE BITS

Bobbins

A long time ago someone - probably Richard Walker... he invented just about everything - had the bright idea of attaching a piece of bread flake to the line between the reel and the butt ring to show bites. This was known as a dough bobbin and usually took the form of a piece of flake squeezed onto the line. Watch the bread. It twitches and moves steadily towards the butt ring... you strike... one carp, thank you very much. Simple ideas are often the best, but it was soon discovered that the bread was not as good an idea as all that. Rats tended to gnaw through the line while they were attacking the bread, and it fell off in the rain. Next trick... silver paper. Same principle, but rain and rat proof.

The silver paper proved perfectly adequate and had a long time as the nation's number one bite indicator... until the men of Kent (not forgetting the Kentish men - I was born there and still don't know the difference) discovered the original Fairy Liquid bottle top. This was clipped to the line to show twitchers and takes and ruled the roost for some time. It had one serious drawback. It blew around all over the place on the breeze. Then someone else - probably Rick Gibbinson... he invented everything else! - came up with the bright idea of running a thin needle through the bottle top and sticking the needle into the ground. Problem solved. From then on it took just a few short steps to arrive at the modern systems.

There are so many indicator bodies on sale these days that it is hard to choose one from another. They all perform the same function to varying degrees... in other words they give a visual back-up to the audible bite alarm to give warning of a take. The body will either move up the needle if a fish is running away from the bank or parallel to it, or it will move down the needle if the fish comes in towards the bank (dropbacks). Bodies come in various sizes, from light plastic ones to two ounce ones used to register the shyest of takes. There are flip top bodies, but basically they all go up and down and register takes.

One thing you don't want is a body that tends to stick to the needle. In the shops, without the tension caused by line running through its hoop, all bodies will appear to perform well, but some can and do stick and may need lubricating. This you do by pouring water down the bore of the body, but this is an annoying chore that shouldn't be necessary, and they can also cost you fish on the bank, because taking fish may well drop a bait if there is too much

An assortment of bobbins.

resistance caused by the body sticking to the needle. They may also fail to show drop backs properly, so if you are not sure how a particular system will perform, get recommendations from other anglers.

Generally the PTFE bodies will prove slick enough, but a little care is needed when choosing any one system. Some that I know work are the ones marketed by Solar Tackle, KJB Products and Leslies of Luton's own adjustable bobbins.

These days I usually carry a wide variety of indicators with me to suit changing circumstances and conditions. For much of my every day fishing, much of which is long range stuff, I now use either the latest Gardner model, the 25 gram GT90's or, if I really want to look the business and do my posing bit, I would choose the new large Lite-Flo indicators from Solar Tackle. These really do look the business. They come in red, green, blue or orange, so if you use Delkims you can match the indicator colour to that of the LED. The effect at night with isotopes inserted has to be seen to be believed, as does the ghostly look of the GT90's. I have found both these indicator models to be very free running on the needle, and have so far experienced no sticking problems at all. I like the flip-top on the GT90's which ensures that the line always comes neatly clear of the needle and the body, even when a fish is really belting off, taking line. I also use the little clear bodied original Gardner monkeys when I need a nice, light and compact body for close-in work.

Recent additions to the tackle shop shelves are the swinging arm type indicators. These comprise a pivoting stainless steel wire arm with a counterbalance weight and a white disc indicator. Fox International's "Swinger Bite Indication System" is one example of this versatile idea. With the counterbalance weight set back to its fullest extent the indicator will show the most delicate of bites. Move the 25 gram weight right forward and the arm becomes heavy enough to show drop-backs at 100 yards plus.

Bank Sticks and Buzzer Bars

The first decent, purpose built banksticks designed with the specimen hunter in mind were the Gardner alloy extending bank sticks. The original ones were much tougher than the alloy ones marketed today, and I still have four of these dating back to '81. After years of being abused and bashed they are still as straight as they ever were and I use them 90% of the time. I have also got a pair of Gardner's stainless outer/alloy inner extenders which I use on gravel pits where a tougher outer is called for. I also use a selection of Gardner's stainless buzzer bars, for while alloy bars are fine for soft ground swims, when you come to push a bankstick into hard gravel using the bar as the pressure point, the bar invariably bends or breaks. Stainless bars are better by far and are not going to bend or fracture. I have found the bankside equipment made by Gardner Tackle totally adequate for all my angling requirements. I have had some of their gear for ten years or more now, and it's still going strong. I have no doubt it will outlast my own angling life.

I would advise anyone thinking of laying out a hundred pounds and more for a set of stainless bars, bank sticks and monkey climber system to stop and consider just how absolutely vital it is for him to carry that considerable extra weight. That said, it has to be admitted that well made stainless systems really do look good. Stainless isn't cheap, but when you consider paying £150 for a rod or £80 for a reel then eleven or twelve quid for a bankstick doesn't seem quite so hard to swallow. Especially when you consider it will last you a lifetime. However, some people think that stainless is for posers and the idea of spending unnecessary sums simply for the sake of posing on the bankside may not make a lot of sense. On the other hand there are waters where a stainless system is very big asset... namely on gravel pits and other hard banked waters.

For instance, in most of the swims at Savay the bank is made up of quite large gravel stones. While it may not be too hard getting the banksticks in, it can be a nightmare getting them in solidly enough, and bobbin needles go wherever they'll fit. Not ideal by any means. Martin Locke's (Solar Tackle) stainless systems are very popular on the lake and with good reason. Simply put, they are robust, efficient and ideal for the tough gravel banks. Solar's Satellite Monkey Climb System is excellent, as are their adjustable buzzer bars and banksticks. Though I haven't used them myself, from what I've seen on the bankside the stainless bankside gear marketed by Leslie's of Luton and Terry Eustace's range look sturdy and efficient.

Just a quickie about rod rest heads themselves. There are a great many on the market and they aren't too expensive. I love the neat and tidy ones from Terry Eustace's Gold Label range. Others worth mentioning are those from

Gardner Tackle and John Roberts and Kingfisher International, but look out for the soon to be introduced stainless rear rests from Solar Tackle. For really secure rear rests you can't beat the Fox Rod Loks. These grip the rod butt tightly between two foam-lined sprung jaws. Perfect for those situations where you are fishing tight to snags and cannot give line.

Finally a word on rod pods. Some fishing situations pose problems with wooden platforms and rock hard or concrete banks. A rod pod will support both front and rear rests, and the additional aerial (or needle bar) will hold the monkey climbers and bobbins in a firm and fixed position. Gardner led the way with two low budget models, which has now been added to with their Mega-Pod and Pro-Pod versions, but there are now several versions on the market, and the KJB Rod-Pod looks and feels a quality item. Many tackle shops also market much of their own purpose built bankside bits including rod pods. These are often made by a local toolmaker and may not be nationally available.

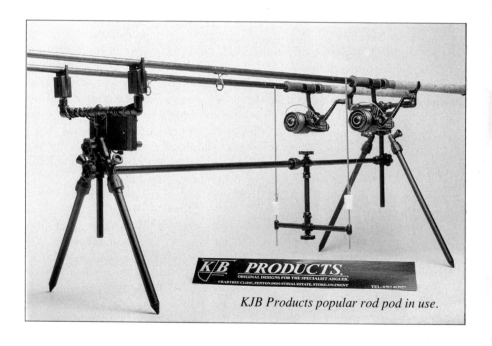

KJB Products popular rod pod in use.

Luggage

That short heading covers a mountain of gear! Only personal choice will dictate your requirements and sort out what is necessary and what is not. There really is so much specialist luggage on offer in the shops that space limits the amount of coverage I can give, but I guess that most carp anglers will need both a rod holdall of some sort and a decent sized rucksack.

I carry most of my tackle in one of the capacious Nash Hooker Rucksacks. These really do hold a tremendous amount but while they are good, they are not that good. Invariably the one item you need here and now will be right at the bottom of the main part and everything has to come out. I think it would be a lot better split into two sections like the Wychwood Rucksack. There are also a vast number of other bags and rucksacks on the market to suit all pockets and occasions. I use a Nash Carp Carryall for all my bedding, cooking and spare clothes, while the bedchair goes in one of the E.T. purpose built bedchair carriers... a very useful bit of gear.

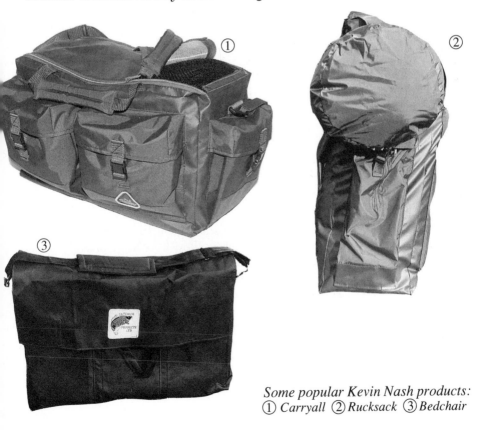

Some popular Kevin Nash products:
① *Carryall* ② *Rucksack* ③ *Bedchair*

Look after your carp.
Shaun Harrison of Walkers
of Trowell demonstrates the
right way to do it with a
superb common.

Most carp anglers prefer to leave their rods made up between sessions and the specialist rod holdalls now on the market allow for this by providing reel pockets and interior ties to secure the rods during transit. I suppose the most popular would be the Nash Hooker Holdall, but there are great many to choose from and it's really question of you pays yer money and you takes yer choice. The E.T. Holdall has so many pockets and zips I reckon items of tackle could be lost without trace within its vast interior. Rod Hutchinson's High Protection line looks really good: a real quality product.

Though not strictly luggage as such, you will need a box of some sort in which to carry the nuts and bolts of carp fishing. The plastic cantilever boxes are a good idea, but you can just as easily get away with a selection of Tupperware or plastic boxes.

Chairs and Bedchairs

If you aren't going to sleep at the lake, I see little point in carrying a bulky bedchair around with you. You'll be far better off with a simple framed garden chair from one of the D.I.Y. superstores. Cheap and cheerful and reasonably comfortable, they do the job well on short sessions. Even on longer trips you may like to take some other form of seating apart from your bedchair, especially on the more "social" lakes, where it just isn't done to turn up without a guest chair and cup! The specialist camping shops also sell low chairs and they are often cheaper than the so-called angler's chairs sold in the tackle shops. The French camping gear manufacturer Lafuma make what is arguably

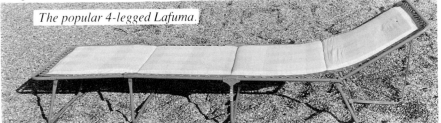

The popular 4-legged Lafuma.

the most comfy, light low chair but shop around and you'll see that there's plenty of choice on the market.

Bedchairs are another kettle of fish. Cheap and cheerful just won't do here. When I think of how I tortured my back sleeping on those ridiculous supermarket garden loungers! I know they are cheap, but when you think how quickly most of us wear the ratchets out (rendering them useless) you're far better off with a proper bed/bedchair.

Carole and I now use Fox bedchairs on all our sessions. I have lost count of the times when I've blessed my Super Deluxe Bedchair. I know a hundred and seventy quid is a lot to pay but when I count the hours I've spent on it, then I regard it as money well spent. The sprung foam-filled mattress and the extra width of 26" suit my build perfectly and of course the adjustable legs are a blessing on awkwardly shaped banks. Carole prefers the standard Bow Frame Bedchair, with its non-sprung canvas cover. It is much firmer and slightly narrower and lighter, but still features the adjustable legs.

Before I got the Fox I used a four leg Lafuma. This is another sprung mattressed bed and is just as comfy as the Fox, but it is restricted in where you can use it. The bank has to be more or less flat and level to accommodate the four frames that form the supports, and it is so low that my old back was finding it more and more difficult to straighten and get me upright after a runless night's kip. However, the Lafuma represents excellent value for money for those agile souls who can manage to get up from six inches off the deck!

Groundsheets and Clothing

The great enemies of the long-session carp angler are cold and damp. You'd be surprised just how much damp comes up from the ground, even during the summer months, yet I still see a lot of younger, inexperienced anglers fishing without a groundsheet. The Bob Frost model that we use is good and waterproof and tear resistant, and it certainly keeps the creeping dampness from spreading upwards. Most of the better tackle and camping shops sell groundsheets of various shapes, sizes and thicknesses, and they really are a must for any overnight fishing trip. In addition I always use a camping roll between the sleeping bag and bedchair. All good camping shops sell them for just a few pounds, and the extra warmth and damp protection they offer are priceless.

Good waterproof clothing helps defeat the elements. I am currently using the new Stalker Products' thermal gear. This is because I'm impressed by the advertising which states… "now worn by the Country's Top Anglers - and Rob Heald". Poor old Rob, but then what did I ever do to deserve the former accolade! Seriously though, the two piece, olive green garments are stylish and very warm, and I like the practicality of the two pieces (think about it!) providing the overlap between top and bottom is good and deep; which it is. In the past I used a Dane Valley one-piece thermal, which served me well for many seasons.

I wear Damart thermal underwear, and tee shirts, plus a hooded sweatshirt under the Stalker gear, and even in the depths of winter I haven't been cold at all, even in -6 degrees.

Proper waterproofs and thermal winter boots are essential for cold weather carping. I like Derry Boots in the summer months, but they just can't hack it in the winter. I've used both Skeetex and Boom 80 thermal boots, and apart from their ludicrous appearance both have served me well through some dreadful weather. The Bob Church one piece waterproof suit is perhaps the best known of all the TRULY waterproof outer garments, but I think it is more suited to non-bivvied day sessions, rather than for longer bivvied-up trips. You see, if you sleep in the suit for warmth and then answer the call of the buzzer during an overnight downpour, though it will certainly keep you dry, once the excitement is all over, the suit has to come off before you can get back into the sleeping bag again… whereupon you get cold! If on the other hand you only wear the suit to go out in the rain, you will spend many precious minutes struggling into it while the carp perhaps makes it to the sanctuary of the snags or whatever.

I prefer the light two-piece Dartex or Gortex waterproofs, which are quick to slip on and off, and are light and compact while still being reasonably

*The excellent
Trangia stove.*

waterproof. I slip the overtrousers down over the boots so that on those rare occasions when I'm roused from my bed by a run, all I need do is step into the boots and pull up the trousers. It only takes seconds and the same goes for the jacket, allowing you to be on the rods with the minimum delay.

Plentiful supplies of hot drinks and food keep the inner man's boilers well stoked and that means you'll need some type of cooker. The camping gas cylinders are O.K. at a push, but in winter the cold weather knocks their pressure right down and they can take forever to make a cup of tea. The American Coleman stoves work on special fuel, and even lead free petrol, and they certainly kick out some heat. For the most part they are reliable, but I've seen some pretty frightening bonfires caused by mishandling. I have used one of the Swedish Trangia metholated spirits burners for several years now. They are totally reliable, and while not as fast as the Coleman burners, they are quick enough for me, boiling a pint of water in about 5 minutes. They have one curious advantage over most other stoves. Due to a rather clever system that funnels the slightest breeze into the stove below the burner, this means that the harder the wind blows the better they work.

Finally don't forget to wear some sort of headgear. Remember you loose 30% of your body heat through your head, so just keeping it covered goes a long way towards maintaining warmth and comfort.

IN THE TACKLE BOX

Hooks

Here's a mind blowing selection. I suppose hooks really should be looked at in relation to rigs, and as I'm only going to touch briefly on rigs themselves in the tactics section, I'll simply mention a few of my own favourite patterns and leave Alan Tomkins to deal with the "horses for courses" aspect of hook selection in his "End Tackle" book which is part of this series.

First off I have to tell you that I always use barbless hooks. Not everyone's cup of tea I know, but I think I can honestly say that I have never lost a fish BECAUSE I was using barbless. I think the advantages far outweigh the disadvantages, and I also think they are more humane in that lost fish can rid themselves of a barbless hook much easier than they can a barbed one. I'm sure we've all seen some terribly deformed mouths on carp that have been caught many times, and barbless hooks allow easier removal, and of course easier penetration in the first place. The range of barbless hooks on the market isn't great and this means that I usually squeeze the barbs flat with pliers.

At present I am using two Partridge patterns for much of my fishing. The Arrowpoint is a barbless pattern but with a curious diamond shaped point which seems to work in much the same way as a barb. They are a curious shape, rather like a nymph fly hook, but they do appear to prick and penetrate well, with considerable strength when a bit of bullying is called for. The other pattern I like is the new Hutchinson hook. The offset eye and long point make them ideal for the "swimmer" rig that allows a correctly balanced bait to be fished tight to the bottom rather than popped up. Incidentally, this is how I fish the Arrowpoints as well as pop-ups are the kiss of death on the waters I fish nowadays. (see diagram 1).

No look at hooks would be complete without considering the superb Drennan Super Specialist. I hate to think how many carp have fallen to these hooks over the years. They are a simple, yet strong and sharp hook and I've always got a selection in my hook box. Other popular hooks are the Owner, Gamakatsu and Kamasan ranges from Japan, but I cannot speak for their efficiency as I've not used them. Enough top class anglers do however, so that speaks for itself doesn't it?

I suppose I should deal with bent hooks. Much has been written about this infamous rig. It is banned on some waters for reasons that escape me, though excessive mouth damage is usually cited as the main reason. My problem with the bent hook is that I cannot get on with it in barbless form. It must be something to do with the downturned eye, the long bent shank and the angle of pull but I keep losing fish on them. However, as I always fish barbless I don't

For use with Partridge Arrowpoint or Partridge Hutchinson. Tie buoyant bait to tiny brass ring with floss and counter balance with tungsten pully. (Swimmer Rig).

Kryston Silkworm 8lb or 15lb b.s.

use the bent hook at present. What I do use is the Gibbinson extension with a barbless size 6 Jack Hilton hook which works just fine. (see diagram 2).

I'm still not sure about outpoint hooks. Sure, they should prick more fish in theory, but do they? I'm not yet convinced, and I was disappointed to note that the new Partridge Piggyback bent hook had an outpoint. Just looking at the rig again I would have thought that it would be better with an inturned point, but again that's only a theory. I have used the Maddocks Cassien Outpoints in the past and caught fish on them, but the points do get weakened when I try to flatten the barbs and most of them snap off. I don't think outpoint and barbless go together anyway, so they've been dropped for the time being.

Gibbinson's line aligner rig.
Brilliant alternative to bent hook rig.

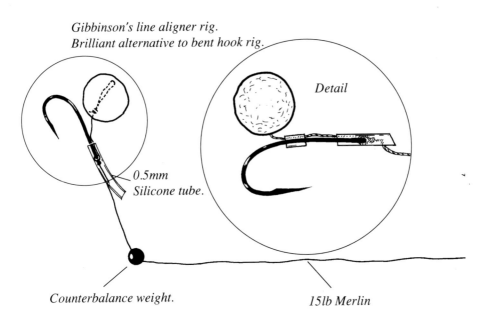

Detail

0.5mm
Silicone tube.

Counterbalance weight.

15lb Merlin

Line

Not too much to say here really. For years I used nothing but Maxima. This is a top quality line sold in bulk spools for better economy and reel loading. It is perfect for all soft bottomed waters but I don't think it stands up to gravel as well as other makes. The other popular line is of course Sylcast, but I've gone off this line these days as it seems to come in an awful shiny bronze colour, which I don't like one bit. I'm not sure if they've changed the dye but it's nothing like the old sorrel colour. I now prefer either Brent Nylon or Simpsons' Carpcatcher line, which is much more like the original Sylcast.

Much of my fishing is done at extreme range on Savay and other big pits these days. This means I need a shock leader to take the power surge of casting and to stand up to the abrasive nature of the lake bed, with a much lighter main line of usually 6-8lbs. I have been using the new Terry Eustace Trilene Big Game line for several months now, and I can honestly say that it's everything Terry claims it to be. Its abrasion resistant qualities are amazing and in France last year I used the twelve pound line right through on a horrendously boulder strewn lake without wearing out the line at all. It also seems to withstand casting shocks much better than any other line I've used.

You might imagine that less expensive lines don't match up to their dearer counterparts in any respect... but you'd be wrong. I can thoroughly recommend the Southern Lines Golden Marlin nylon, particularly in the heavier breaking strains. Where else can you get 1750 yards of 8lbs breaking strain, quality German nylon for just over four quid! Its abrasion resistance isn't as good as the Trilene, but it's every bit as good as Maxima and Sylcast.

Finally, a mention of the new ultra fine nylons such as Drennan's Double Strength. To be honest I cannot see any advantage in these lines as far as carp fishing is concerned. Their lack of stretch means their impact strength is reduced, and they seem excessively prone to tangling when used as a reel line for long distance work. The only application I can see for them is as hooklinks, and there they have to match up to the modern braids such as Kryston's Super Silk - which they fail to do.

I don't want to say too much about hooklink materials. After all, they are more related to rigs which are being discussed in another book. So apart from mentioning the superb modern braids such as Silkworm, Merlin and Super Silk from Kryston, and of course the superb Kryston Multistrand - not forgetting Nashy's Gamabraid and Gamastrand, I'll leave the subject to Alan Tomkins.

Other Bits and Pieces

I've just about run my course for this section. The amount of new items of carp tackle coming into the tackle shops these days is staggering, and I can't hope to cover it all here. So to finish I just want to list the bits and pieces I carry around in my tackle box that I feel are essential and leave you to think it over and form your own opinion.

CATAPULTS & THROWING STICKS

The Jumbo Cobra throwing stick is an essential piece of my tackle. With practice an 18mm boilie can be thrown well over 100 yards. A pouch catapult will be required for close range baiting up with particles, but for longer distances I'd suggest either a particle dropper (also known as a spod) such as Gardner's Bait Rocket, or the Cobra Groundbaiter.

I've heard that many English anglers are having problems with this, which seems strange to me. The Europeans can't get enough of them! Admittedly the Groundbaiter demands a bit of thought and application to get the best from it but it is worth it. Briefly the Groundbaiter is a spoon-shaped scoop that screws into a landing net handle. With practice it can be used to put groundbait or particles out fifty yards or more. The diagram explains how to get the best from it.

I have just been looking at the latest King Cobra throwing stick. The stick is basically a longer version of the best selling Cobra No. 2 stick. The extra length means extra weight which in turn leads to extra impetus and longer distance. Good thinking Nina!

Cobra Jumbo (left) and King Cobra.

Cobra Groundbaiter.

Sacks, Weigh Slings and Scales

I carry three Nash Zip sacks, but I've modified them by cutting off both bottom corners. This gives access to the sacked up fish of a constant supply of fresh water. That's vital, particularly in warm weather conditions when sacking can be a dodgy business due to oxygen depletion in the sack. In practice you'll find that carp soon find the corner and stick their mouths through the hole. I've also replaced the securing string with a longer, more substantial length of $1/_4$" polypropylene rope. PLEASE, PLEASE ensure that the sack is properly secured to the bank. Wherever possible I like to tie my sacks to a branch or the tree itself, hence the polyprop. rope. Otherwise secure to a deeply pushed-in bank stick or sack pegs. You cannot take too much trouble to make sure the sack is properly secured. Imagine the horror of the slow death suffered by a carp drifting around the lake, unable to escape the

A carp sack is a useful item of tackle on waters where their use is permitted. But never do this - put 2 carp in one sack, as shown in this specially posed shot.

deadly confines of the unsecured sack.

I've got a couple of slings, one of which doesn't get much use. It's a Nash Big Sling meant for those real lunkers, and I don't catch many of them. I also use one of the very good E.T. weigh slings. Scales are the new 40lb Avons, and if I ever catch a bigger fish than that I'll have to go on the cadge to find someone with a set of the Nash Hooker scales that weigh up to 56lbs. If they're not good enough I'll have died and gone to heaven, or I'm dreaming again!

PVA String
(I use Gardner's). For making stringers, which not only help prevent tangles but are a highly effective presentation in their own right.

Tubing
Of all sorts of bores, stiffness and thickness. I like the Terry Eustace and the Gardner silicone and plastic tubing best.

Swivels
Must be Berkley, though to be honest even those aren't really reliable when it comes to preventing tangles, but they are at least very strong for their size. Frankly I've yet to find a swivel that actually swivels!

Tungsten Putty
For counterbalancing/balancing buoyant hookbaits. Again, Gardner for me.

Leads
Zipp leads are no better in my book than ordinary bombs. I can't see the point in paying extra for a fancy name. If using swivelled leads, always make sure the swivel is buried in the body of the lead so that it almost covers the barrel. The whole range sold under the Gardner banner are well designed and thought out, with a tough, reliable swivel. I like the Nash Bolt Leads, but they are too bulky to cast all that far, while the new vogue for round leads such as the Gardner and Nash ones are designed to be thrown in by hand... joke! What I mean is that they don't cast at all. Good idea though for heavy shock rigs.

Power Gum
For stop knots and other rig applications.

Hair Stops
I refuse to buy those carded shop bought ones. Who actually buys these things??? Surely you've enough imagination to find your own for free. Also small strips of buoyant foam can be used as boilie stops and will counterbalance hooks at the same time.

Landing Nets
I use Gardner 42" arms with a Dual Mesh Kevin Nash net. A Terry Eustace Alloy screw-in spreader block fits the end of a standard Dinsmore's 6 foot landing net handle. You can pay a small fortune for a complete landing net system. If you think it's justifiable spending £70 plus for a net by all means do so. Personally I can't see the point and am quite happy with the net I use.

KNIVES, SCISSORS & FORCEPS

Ultra sharp for cutting the modern braids and multistrands. I carry a pair of 8" curved artery forceps, but these are really a throwback to those distant days when I used barbed hooks. I've seen some right botch-ups on the bankside as inept carp anglers struggle to unhook fish. If the hook won't come out the way it went in, even with forceps, bring the point through the flesh and get hold of it with the forceps and pull it through. You'll obviously need to cut the hooklink but it's better than destroying the poor carp's mouth. Alternatively, use barbless hooks which just slip out, causing almost no damage or distress.

BEADS

Many sizes including large bore and shock-absorbent rubber beads.

HAIR NEEDLES, STRINGER NEEDLES ETC.

Self explanatory, Look in wool shops for knitting machine needles. Just like the Waters Edge ones.

STORM RODS AND BOLTS

From the Nash stable for extra security on the forward stress-bearing type bivvies.

Storm caps and their use.

DENTAL FLOSS

For tying buoyant baits to the modern critically balanced rigs. I like the waxed types, and I can't help wondering if the peppermint flavoured, waxed green floss from Johnson & Johnson isn't an attractor in its own right.

Oh hell! there's so much I don't know where to stop. I could keep adding bits all day. Let's stop now and get onto the tactical applications of all this stuff!

TACTICS

I've had to give considerable thought to the compilation of this section on carp angling tactics, simply because I have been asked to write about tactical considerations OTHER THAN rigs and bait. Now if you think about your own standard tactical approach for a moment, you may well find that these two subjects dominate your thinking. But think about it for a moment. Surely the best bait ever on the craftiest rig known since the dawn of time will still catch you nothing if you ain't on carp... And that's what this section will concentrate on to a large degree. Finding the little devils in the first place.

But before we go any further, I'd like to kick off this part of the book by asking a question. Namely...

"What do you expect from your carp fishing?"

Daft question to ask... it's obvious ain't it? Bloody great carp cradled in my arms, spreading the sweet slime of success all over my jumper. That's what I expect! O.K. That's an obvious, though rather simplistic answer, but I'd argue that the question might need further thought. First of all you have to ask yourself how much time you are willing to devote to your passion (I'm talking about carp fishing stupid!). It is all too easy to fall into one of angling's little traps.

You open the weeklies... there's Maylin or MacDonald, Little or Hutchinson plastered all over the pages with another great big beastie. Why can't I catch fish like that? you ask yourself, unaware, or maybe ignoring the fact that they might have spent a month or even a year or more after that one fish. Can you devote that amount of time to your fishing?

I suppose it must appear that all carp fishing nowadays is long session, wear 'em down stuff. Indeed, that may be the case on some waters. I know the most successful anglers on Longfield didn't just count the days between runs... they counted the WEEKS, and in some cases even the years! I understand the Yateley fish have become just as hard to catch, and I've spent more than one completely blank week at Savay. So put things into perspective. If you are prepared to sacrifice a normal every day life for a few big fish that's fine. But be aware that jobs have been lost and even marriages wrecked by such fanatical pursuit. On the other hand, I see nothing wrong in really going for something that you want out of life... always providing that others don't get hurt in the process.

If, like me, you are one of these long session anglers you will have more opportunity to catch fish than your less fortunate brothers, who can perhaps only manage every other weekend. You will catch more fish than them, but that does not make you a better angler. All you have is more time to follow the passion. I've often said in past articles that the longer I have stayed on a water, not necessarily in the same swim, the better my fishing has become. The long session man has more opportunity to spot moving fish, to establish a bait and to build up a swim. That said, there are among us a select few who need none of these advantages to catch fish. Unfortunately we can't all be members of this rare breed.

If we consider the number of regular carp anglers now fishing in the UK and assume an arbitrary figure of, say, 50,000. How many of them do you think would be what we might term "full time" anglers? I'd guess it's not more than 2-3%. There are others who are self employed who make up their own minds just how much time they can devote to the passion, but for the most part, it is the normal 9-5 working man who forms the majority of the carp fishing fraternity. He has only limited time to go fishing; may be married with kids and all the responsibilities that a family entails. It would therefore be wrong of him to expect to match the results of the more fortunate "full timers".

So be realistic and keep an open mind when you read of some so-called superstar's bumper season. Remember that the idea of carp fishing is TO HAVE FUN! I can speak from experience here and can tell you without fear of contradiction that you can't have fun if you keep putting yourself under pressure to catch more and bigger fish. A few years back a common phenomenon called "The Numbers Game" pervaded carp fishing. It caused jealousy, bitterness, extreme secrecy, violence and depression... all for the sake of a few carp. I'd hoped it had disappeared for good, but sadly it seems to be creeping back into modern day carp fishing. Newcomers should be aware of this creeping malaise and guard well against it. I can vouch for the fact that it just ain't worth it.

So where does all that leave Mr. Average, with say just weekends and maybe pre and post-work sessions? Well not as badly off as the proceeding paragraphs may at first have suggested.

I believe that many long stay carp fishers suffer from being too stereo-typed in their approach. The Three B's (buzzers, bivvies and boilies) attitude is all too easy to follow, and it can be efficient way to catch carp. But total reliance on just one method of fishing can also cost you fish. It's all too easy to tell oneself that there's plenty of time... the bait won't really be working yet... let them come to me. The anglers with time on their hands get good at doing nothing, and that's not conducive to catching carp. I'm sure there are a great many carp anglers who have, at times, felt a certain dissatisfaction at the way they are fishing. I've felt this lethargy myself and have had to force myself to do something... even if it's just making a cup of tea or tying spare rigs. Mind you, that's time that would have been better spent watching the water, or stalking fish. The trouble is that on long sessions it is quite possible for laziness to set in.

The short session man shouldn't suffer from any such problems. With only limited time on his hands he'll probably work harder at his fishing, will be more efficient and, pro rata, may well catch more fish. I'm sure there's many a long-stay carp man who's been reduced to tears when a weekender turns up in the next swim and pulls a hatful of carp from the water he's been blanking all week.

This is all part of the question I posed earlier about what an individual wants from his fishing. In the past I was convinced I had the patience to sit it out for weeks on end in the hope of a real whacker. Maybe I had the patience, but didn't have the skill to match, and the monsters never came my way. I then realised that I enjoyed catching carp... full stop. If they wagged their tail that was good enough for me. Yes, of course I like to catch big fish, but perhaps I'm living in the wrong part of the country to catch thirties and forties. After all, Cornwall isn't overcrowded with big fish waters, and I'm no different to many of you reading this book in having to travel to find better fishing. So that's another aspect of carping. You must set your sights on realistic targets. Unless you can afford to spend time and money flying down the motorways to the Home Counties, the North West or abroad, don't expect to catch the sort of monsters that constantly figure in the papers. I like to think I have built my reputation (What!) on catching the better fish from the restricted waters I have available to me and I reckon that catching the biggest fish in a pool is a result, no matter whether the fish weighs fourteen pounds or forty.

I think that's more or less enough about attitudes and aspirations. If you are just getting into carp fishing, PLEASE, I beg you, don't try and catch the biggest and the best straight away. It leaves you with nowhere to go; nothing to aspire to. I remember a youngster who'd just caught his very first carp complaining that it was "only fifteen pounds." Boy is that guy in for some hefty disillusion in the years to come... always assuming that he doesn't burn himself out in search of impossible dreams. Believe me, a fifteen pound fish is as worthy an adversary as a five pounder or a twenty five pounder. It's all relative to the water you are fishing and what you want to get out of the sport. Nuff said, yes?

I just want to say a few words about terminal rigs. I shall not be dealing with them to any great extent in this book, for while I accept that they are important, they don't enter into my tactical planning when moving onto a new water until I have answered the more critical questions posed by the lake. For too many anglers the end rig has become a fishing method in itself. They pay little attention to far more important aspects such as watercraft, the weather

or bait. Too often I see inexperienced carp anglers pinning excessive hopes on
the latest rig to catch him fish, without seeing the terminal set-up as part of an
overall picture. Rigs are just a small part that helps to make up the whole.

I also consider that one of the greatest mistakes anyone can make is to
dissociate bait from rig. It is fundamentally clear that the stronger the carp are
feeding on your bait, the less sophisticated your rig needs to be. Just to give
an example of this, I need look no further than the results of my friend Gary
Thomas on some of the waters he fishes. His rigs are simple, basic, and easy
to tie. He uses a very good bait and gets the fish feeding hard on it before
starting fishing, by prebaiting. He catches more fish than most - especially big
fish - and his results speak for themselves.

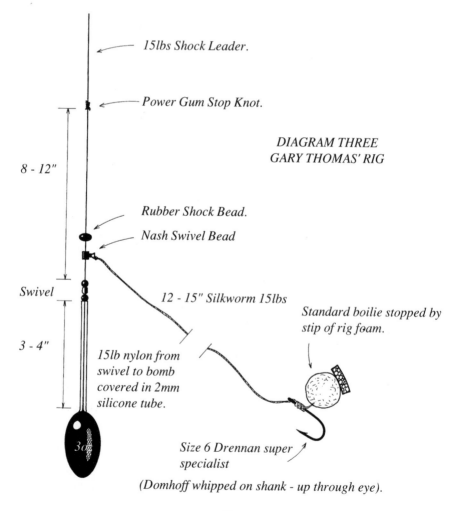

15lbs Shock Leader.

Power Gum Stop Knot.

DIAGRAM THREE
GARY THOMAS' RIG

8 - 12"

Rubber Shock Bead.

Nash Swivel Bead

Swivel

12 - 15" Silkworm 15lbs

Standard boilie stopped by
stip of rig foam.

3 - 4"

15lb nylon from
swivel to bomb
covered in 2mm
silicone tube.

Size 6 Drennan super
specialist

(Domhoff whipped on shank - up through eye).

So you won't find any superduper high-tech, gen kiddie rigs here. (In fact, you'll find these in Alan Tomkin's book in the carpth in depth series). Oh! I agree, it's vital on some waters to get the rig absolutely right. Having the right rig can be the difference between success and failure, and on some of the pressure waters your hook link and/or end rig can make or break your trip but; to be honest, I sometimes think that we set too much store by the importance of what is basically only one individual aspect of carp fishing. While I accept that ultra rig conscious carp do exist, I don't think these 'Brain of Britain' fish aren't as widespread as many would have us believe.

O.K., you're saying, if he doesn't consider rigs to be part of the tactical battle, what the hell is left? Well, quite a lot when you just think about it. Later we'll consider bankside set-ups, the use of backleads, improving or increasing drag or resistance as appropriate, stalking fish, swim choice, effect of wind and atmospheric pressure and, of course, bait application. All these will play a major part in dictating whether you are successful or not, but when it comes right down to it watercraft or, more specifically, location is the most vital ingredient in the recipe for success. You can have the finest bait in the world, on the trickiest rig ever invented, but if you aren't on fish - forget it. This is particularly so on big, open waters where there can be many influencing factors as to where the fish are likely to be found. It's not so hard on small waters, where it's likely there are fish over your baits **at least** once every 24 hours, if not more often.

I think it would be best to consider the various types of aquatic environments that we encounter separately. What might be good tactics for one, might be poor ones for another. I want to deal with three types of lake. Namely, small estate lakes and ponds up to, say, 3-4 acres in size; next we'll look at larger, natural and artificial lakes, meres and reservoirs, such as those found in some parts of France, before finally dealing with perhaps the most common lakes for most of us, gravel pits. Each category presents us with a separate set of problems and each needs to be tackled in a different way.

All of us learn from experience. I have fished quite a few different waters, so in the sections that follow I'll look at my own experiences on a few waters in order to illustrate the points I'm trying to make. All of the waters exist - indeed, some of you may recognise one or two of them, but whether or not you are familiar with these waters, I think I'll feel happier writing specifically, rather than in generalities.

But first, before we go any further, I would like to consider the effect of the weather upon carp and the waters they inhabit. Wind, temperature, atmospheric pressure and a lot of other natural phenomena all affect our fishing, and I'm sure I don't have to tell you just how important weather influences can be. That's not to say, of course, that the elements should override other considerations such as, say, food availability, but the successful carp angler needs to learn the lessons that the weather gods can teach us.

THE ELEMENTS: THEIR TACTICAL EFFECTS

Wind

I don't suppose there is an angler among us who would argue that the wind strength and direction can have a profound effect on their fishing. General consensus of opinion will tell you that fresh, warm, south or south westerly winds are the so-called 'feeding winds' and that fish don't feed in northerlies or any wind with east in it. Funny that. I've enjoyed some fantastic fishing in fresh east winds, and I know one water where they always feed on northerlies.

The weather lore continues "It should also be blowing hard if it's going to blow at all - the harder the better".

I fish a water where they appear to hate strong winds! So we should beware of vague generalisations when considering the elements. You just can't make them about so complex a subject. I just wish it **was** all as cut and dried as that. Sadly, it isn't. In fact, there are **many** waters where there is little or no wind effect whatsoever, while on others if can be a crucial factor in fish location.

I have fished College Reservoir, near Penryn, a great deal over the years and have yet to draw any hard and fast conclusion about the effect wind has on that lake. Sometimes the wind can really be hacking into the North Bay on fresh, warm southerlies, yet the fish just don't seem to get caught up there in the teeth of the wind. Rather, they will hang around the islands at the opposite end of the lake with half a gale sweeping over their heads. On paper you'd think that, in the shallow water, every fish in the lake would be on the move, influenced by the pull of the breeze. In reality, this doesn't happen. No, what happens, in effect, is that the wind stimulates the fish into feeding - not where you'd expect them to feed, but where they already know there is food to be found, around the islands. **Not** where you would like them to be feeding, namely, up in the teeth of the breeze.

On the other hand, there is an area called 'The Cut' on College, which is a long narrow finger off the main lake, that leads down to the dam, which runs directly east/west. Here the water is deeper and there is less silt. You would imagine that the carp would not be drawn into this part on strong winds. After all, there is less food and more bankside disturbance, yet on really violent westerly winds, the fish congregate in 'The Cut' and are very catchable. I wish I knew what draws them into this spot in particular, when they don't seem to be influenced by strong winds pushing into the shallower parts of the lake.

Mind you, there are waters where the wind seems to be the sole influencing factor in determining where fish will be feeding. I know most of the Savay syndicate feel the wind plays a vital part in their swim choice and when I first went onto the water I was astonished at the way the lads would be forever moving swims on a shift in the wind. If you read Rod Hutchinson's book, 'The Carp Strikes Back', you'll see just how important Rod felt the right wind to be. Incidentally, Savay is one of the very few waters I know where the fish move on strong north winds, which are usually cold and less conducive to inciting a feeding response.

People will tell you that things have changed at Savay in recent years. Now you'll hear members talking about the negative influence of the breeze; the inference being that the fish have wised up to being pushed around the lake, following the wind. They realised that danger awaited them at the windward end in the form of anglers' baits and, instead, the fish now react by moving **against** the wind!

I must say, I still find this hard to swallow. After all, if the wind direction had been such an influencing factor, then surely it was a natural stimulus that they would find hard to act against. Could it really be possible that the carp could ignore their natural instincts? Indeed, to react in opposition to those instincts?

This year I've had plenty of opportunity to assess these theories for myself. My first trip of the year found me sitting it out in the Cottage Bay, in the teeth of almost continuous southerly winds. I expected fish to be in the bay, but only had two runs, a sixteen pound carp and an eight pound bream. I should have realised from my isolation up there that the rest of the syndicate knew the fish wouldn't be in the bay. They were spread out down the canal bank, away from the breeze, and catching fish.

Next rota and those fickle carp had another good trick to play on me. Similar conditions, wind a fresh to strong south south/west. I looked at The Cottage and remembered my previous mistake. The North Bay was out for the same reason. I lugged all my gear right down to the far end and went in the most southerly swim there, which is called The Sluices. I spent three runless days there before finally twigging that all the fish were in the North Bay and the Cottage! They'd reacted to the breeze in complete contrast to my previous session in the Cottage, two weeks earlier. Sometimes you can't win...

If all that just confuses you more well, I'm sorry, for when things like that happen I'm as confused as you are. Certainly, the way carp react to wind strength and direction is a pretty complicated one.

So, is there any established law governing the way carp move on a wind? Well, I have to say that after 20 years of fishing I have only managed to come up with a few general rules that I feel confident enough to take from water to water and even then I can't rely on them 100%. For what it's worth, here they are.

1. Fish are more **likely** to move on warm winds than on cold ones.
2. If you don't know the water, assume that they **will** be on the end of the wind, until you find out differently.
3. Convince yourself that you are more likely to catch in windy conditions than in flat calm. It isn't always the case, but it's a good rule of thumb.

So you see, it is important that you should know the water you are fishing on and whether the fish are influenced by the breeze or not. It may well be that the fish will box the compass with the wind, or they might only move on a wind from a certain direction. Less likely, but certainly possible, is that they won't be influenced into moving by any breeze at any time, no matter how strong or from what direction. Complicated, ain't it?

On small, deep waters, I find the wind strength and direction becomes less significant. Certainly the really deep waters are not affected to any great extent. On Rashleigh I've known the wind to swing through 180 degrees and then back again in a 24 hour period, and the fish just stayed put on my baits. Rashleigh has depths of up to 40 feet and I was fishing in about 18 feet on a shelf. Perhaps at these depths any influence the wind might have is lost and the carp are not affected at all.

Shallow lakes do seem to be more affected. Salamander Lake has an average depth of only three feet or so. The fish are cute and know it all, but they **always** follow a warm breeze down into the corner by the inlet, where they almost invariably feed, colouring up the water, rolling and bow waving about in the shallow water. I'm sure they are getting a sort of 'fix' on the highly oxygenated water caused by the wave effect of strong winds. There is food a-plenty in the top bay where they end up and I don't think they can help themselves from having a good old nosh up. Mind you, it's one thing to know they'll be there, it's quite another thing to catch them!

I wish I knew why waters react to the wind so differently. The same goes for the fish themselves. There could be any number of reasons. For myself, I tend to think that carp actually 'enjoy' (if that's the right word) the feeling of playing about in wild water. Certainly the increased oxygen levels in the disturbed water off the windward bank must be attractive to them. The discolouration of the water through wave action will also draw fish onto a lee shore, as will the stirred up insect life in the dirty water, but will they still follow the signs if they know there isn't much food up there where the wind is blowing? Surely, the feeding instinct takes precedence over all others. Maybe it's nothing to do with any of these. Perhaps they are reacting to changes in atmospheric pressure that cause the strong winds to blow in the first place.

Temperature

I wasn't sure if temperature warranted a separate heading, so closely tied as it is to the preceding section dealing with the effects of the wind. Indeed, wind and temperatures are practically inseparable, but knowledge of how air and water temperatures can alter carp's behaviour is important. Indeed, it can be critical in deciding whether carp are likely to feed or not.

A strong wind, combined with a low air temperature, may suspend temporarily the carp's inclination to feed as the knock-on effect of lower water temperature is felt. In summer, this may be a short term effect, but in winter they may stop feeding for days on end. Indeed, it is in the coldest months of the year that critical air and water temperatures often govern our chance of a fish or two.

I suppose it is stating the obvious to say that water temperature is directly related to air temperature and wind strength, but have you ever considered that, to a large extent, water temperature is also the carp's natural clock. The temperature of water changes much less rapidly than that of air, so the structure of the carp's environment changes only slowly with the seasons. Water dwelling plants and animals are quite used to these temperature changes and have evolved to adapt to them gradually as the year progresses.

Steve Bennett with a lovely twenty caught at sixty yards range.

However, the effect of warm and cold winds, and their accompanying cool or warm air temperatures is obvious.

I have found that carp are likely to feed longer and harder on rising water temperatures than they are on falling ones during settled conditions, particularly in winter. On the other hand, there are waters where carp feed well just after a big freeze up has occurred and, in fact, the Savay lads will tell you that the **approach** of freezing weather is also known to trigger a feeding response from the lake's carp. How the carp know, I'm not sure. Perhaps it could be some sort of instinctive natural response to a prolonged drop in water temperature, combined with a rise in atmospheric pressure and a probable decrease in wind strength. Remember that most severe frosts occur in anti-cyclonic conditions where, as a rule, the airs are light and the skies are clear. The sun's inclination above the horizon on the shortest day is only eleven degrees, so even on a cloudless day with unbroken sunshine, in December it has little or no effect on water temperatures. At night, the air temperature drops rapidly, there is usually little breeze and the pressure will often rise to well over 1040 millibars. Could the approach of this combination of weather conditions herald the much vaunted feeding spell?

I have to admit that I am somewhat sceptical about the link between approaching frosts and a feeding spell. In fact, I have never found it to work for me and I've fished in some pretty cold weather in my time. I cannot see the logic in it. If carp were so worried about the arrival of extreme cold, why not wait until the lake has frozen over completely? Carp are known to feed under the ice and have even been caught through holes in the ice. Why should they then be concerned about the approach of a freeze up when the ice will form a comparatively warm insulating blanket over the lake?

Water is at its most dense at a temperature of 3.94 degrees C., but it freezes at 0 degrees. This means that ice is less dense than water at just above zero, which is why it floats. It follows therefore that the water under the ice will be warmer and denser and the reason why carp are able to survive under a blanket of ice. The colder water is also able to maintain a high level of oxygen so the fish are in no danger of suffocating through deoxification.

I like to carry a water thermometer with me, especially in winter. I don't consider it as vital as I once did, when there were times when I wouldn't even cast out if the water temperature was too low! Nowadays I use it to look for warmer areas of water within a lake. Carp will often lie up in water only a degree or so warmer than the majority of the lake and may stay in one area all winter. These warmer spots are often found in naturally fed waters where the spring water coming up from below may be warmer. Many stream fed lakes will have their warmer water at the inlet end, though any temperature differences will be quickly dissipated as the lake absorbs the stream water. Deeper waters can sometimes be warmer than the surface levels but the effect of strong winds can wipe out any difference very quickly. The popularity of the much loved 'deep 'ole' is, I believe, overplayed. By mid winter the temperature of the water is more or less the same throughout, so it pays to spend some time trying to find slightly warmer areas.

One lake I fish has a large artificial waterfall emptying into it. The water from this is always a degree or two higher than the lake water and there are always carp to be found swimming around at the foot of the falls. That carp like artificial warm water outlets is well known, and pretty obvious really. The famous Electricity Cut at Peterborough, and the warm water outlets on the Twente Canal in Holland, are just two examples that spring to mind.

As the summer approaches, the lake and its inhabitants are stirred into life by the warming water temperatures. Foodstuff production improves, weed growth is increased and the carp are usually triggered into spawning activity. Though temperature change in summer may not be so critical as in the winter months, it can play a big part in determining where the carp are likely to be found. In deep lakes, the bottom layers warm up less slowly than the upper layer and will also hold less oxygen as the warmer temperatures set off decomposition of dead material that has sunk to the bottom. Carp don't like decomposing rubbish and will move onto the warmer, better oxygenated shallower parts of the lake, or into the upper layers over deep water where they will feel more comfortable.

On the other hand, in shallow lakes, the wave and wind action will stir the lake water right through and their temperatures remain constant from surface to bottom. This stirring of the lake water means that the nutrients are released from the lake bed for re-use, and thus shallow lakes will be found to be much more productive than deep ones.

I could go on at great length about the effects of temperature; I find the subject fascinating. I am sure that I have caught many of my better fish by following my instincts governed by considerations of air and water temperature and I'm sure it would pay you to read up as much as you can on the subject.

Other Weather Imponderables

I've mentioned atmospheric pressure in passing a couple of times now. I have been aware of its importance in fishing ever since I first went to sea as a commercial fisherman. In the U.K., high pressure usually means calm or easterly winds and poor fishing. Low pressure the exact opposite. I was sure when I came ashore that this knowledge should apply to freshwater fish and fishing.

I am not sure whether it is due to the dreaded 'greenhouse effect', but here in Britain we seem to be suffering from weather extremes these past few years. One particular low pressure area that passed to the north of Scotland had a barometric centre of 940, if memory serves me well. That is what I call a low pressure area! When I was at sea, the weather was of prime importance in deciding if I could earn a crust or not. Consequently, I kept a close eye on the weather patterns. I can never recall a low pressure area like that, nor the correspondingly high pressure of last summer (1990) when the pressure soared over the 1050 mark. (It was a bit hot too, if you remember!). Now as I write in February, 1991, the country is in the grip of another European high of above 1050, bringing bitter Siberian weather.

Now as a rule, high pressure means light winds and clear skies, while low pressure brings cloud, rain and wind. We have already seen the effect of strong, warm winds and it is no coincidence that they occur with low pressure areas. However, can we be sure that we **know** which influence it is that the carp are reacting to? I do know they are reacting to **something**! My experiences over the years have only served to confirm my belief that changes in atmospheric pressure affect the feeding patterns of carp, and I have found this to be so right throughout the year.

So, though you may find it a lot more pleasant fishing during the quiet, still heat of a summer anti-cyclone, you will almost certainly catch more in the blood and guts of a rain lashed southerly gale. Here's one other observation that seems to hold true 90% of the time - carp tend to feed more on falling pressure than on rising.

That's enough about pressure. What else might influence carp and carp fishing? Here's where I go off into the realms of the unknown and probably unprovable.

I am sure the moon affects carp fishing and not just by its light. (I don't know about you, but I've never done well when there's been a big, full moon beaming down from a cloudless sky). I am convinced that the moon's gravitational pull must also have an effect even on fresh waters. On full and new moons, the tides are at their strongest (the spring tides). Twice every month there occurs a period when two thirds of the earth's surface is being pushed and pulled around the globe by forces the strength of which we can only guess at. Is it stretching credibility too far to think that this colossal force and movement doesn't affect fresh water as well as salt?

We first fished College on the very big springs of 23rd/24th October, 1983. We caught a barrel of fish. Things then went quiet for a couple of weeks until the next springs arrived. On the 23rd/24th and 25th November, we fished again on big tides and had another beano. Then it went quiet again until the new moon springs. By the full moon springs at Christmas, the fish were ready for another pasting and Steve Westbury had five or six fish in about four hours' fishing. Coincidence? Maybe - but it still works for me, even today. Could it be because the water is less than a mile from the sea?

I've probably said too much about the elements but, believe me, they are important. Talk to any of the top flight carp anglers and ask them if they listen

No need to tell you what the conditions were like here! Ken with a wet weather biggie of thirty pounds plus.

regularly to forecasts, or move on the strength of a warm summer breeze. I would be lost without the shipping forecasts which are more detailed and far more accurate than the general forecasts, as well as giving atmospheric pressure and barometric rises and falls.

You can't do anything to change the weather, but you can make it work for you and steal a march on those who never consider its effects.

TACTICAL CONSIDERATIONS

I wonder what you'd consider as the most important feature that goes towards making a particular swim a 'hot' one. Would you say the presence of a bar or a plateau? Maybe regular introductions of artificial bait? Perhaps it's underwater currents, a stream bed, the way the wind funnels through the swim - all these and more may play their part, but the overriding factor that makes a swim a good 'un is the presence of natural food, and in large quantities.

Food is the key to catching carp. Not so much of your own offerings of bait (though of course this is very significant when building up a swim), but the insect and plant life that fish need to survive. Carp are highly skilled in detecting natural food vial olfactory stimuli (smell in human terms), and if you can find where they are feeding, then the job's at least half done.

Before you even start fishing any new water, be it large or small, gravel pit or farm pond, you must first do some basic groundwork. You cannot expect good catches if the preparation work has been slapdash or, worse, non-existent. It's not a lot of good going into a known hot swim if you are only using other people's experiences in it to guide you (although of course these will certainly help you as I'll explain later on). You must do your own planning to get the best out of it.

The things you need to know about the water are fairly obvious when you come to think about it. For instance, we have already talked about the weather influences, so try and find out if the fish follow the wind. Spend as much time as you possibly can just sitting quietly by the lake with a pair of binoculars, watching for sings of moving fish. You will be surprised how quickly you can learn and identify possible patrol routes and feeding areas, even at long range. The best time to get this detail firmly in your mind is during the close season, when the lake will be quieter, the fish under no angling pressure, and most probably feeding hard.

Prior to, and just after, spawning, carp feed avidly on anything they can find that is edible. Their need for energy at this stressful time of the year forces them into a slightly unnatural pattern of feeding and they will often betray their presence over areas of high natural food density by leaping, colouring up the bottom and other obvious displays. These spots must be pinpointed, for while this aberrant feeding behaviour may not be prolonged, there may well come a time during the year when carp will move onto one of these areas, either due to angling pressure or weather influences. On waters that are subjected to greater than average angling pressure, carp will often stop feeding on the known pressure hot spots and adopt totally new feeding patterns. One example of this occurred for us at Waveney Valley Lakes in the autumn of 1984.

Carole and I had fished 'C' Lake for the best part of a week, casting across to the far bank treeline as tight as possible to the distant margin. All summer carp had been making mistakes right along the treeline, but this week it seemed as if they had suddenly stopped picking up baits completely in the danger zone. Now there are an awful lot of carp in 'C' Lake, to say nothing of a big head of bream, and this fact, plus a recent stocking with new 'green' carp, straight from the stock pond, should at least have provided some signs of life, but for ten days or more, with every caravan full and most of the bivvy swims occupied, not a fish was caught on the lake. This was really strange, for the fish showed regularly all over the lake and were plainly feeding hard on natural food items, but their treeline nervousness appeared to have affected them to such an extent that they weren't picking up baits at all.

Carole and I were perhaps lucky in that we were in caravan 18. The swim is unique, in that it has one of the very few gravel bars in it. It is only a very small one, but is an easily detected area of fairly clean gravel about thirty yards out, and I felt sure they must feed there at times.

We started a light baiting programme in the hope of attracting the obviously feeding carp, but we couldn't risk spooking them in any way. The bait we introduced, therefore, was in paste form, containing no artificial attractors at all, as the carp might recognise these and refuse the bait. Instead, we used an amino acid combination in crystal form as the only natural signal from the bait. We baited up at regular intervals with freshly made pastes, the thinking being that even if we weren't getting action from the carp, the bream would eat the pastes and stop any suspicious build up of uneaten bait on the bar (see diagram 4 on page 58).

Anyway, to get to the nub of the issue. Using small, boiled baits with stringers attached, we suddenly found action in no uncertain manner. We finished our week with eleven fish on the bank out of fourteen takes and, during one brief spell of madness, had four out and lost one in less than an hour. I think most of the other anglers on the lake blanked and the only other fish to come out were taken well away from the treeline.

So I hope you see what I mean about identifying possible alternative feeding areas for those odd times when the hot spots die on you, due solely to the pressure. It may well be that the fish won't visit these areas often, nor feed there for long, but your bait stands every chance of tempting them into a mistake if they are not used to seeing bait there. Indeed, having found a spot where carp do feel confident of picking up baits, it may well be that you can keep this swim going for quite a while with a 'little but often' baiting campaign.

Finding hot spots in a large lake may not be easy. There will be parts of the lake where the fish are quite happy to laze about, possibly even to show themselves, but they don't feed in them. They are simply holding areas, perhaps with little natural food in them. I can't emphasise enough that in order to find angling hot spots, you must find the food larders which carp use naturally from habit. These will be visited by feeding fish on a regular basis, and proper bait application to the right spot should bring results. Indeed, you don't need to build a bait mountain in order to be successful. If you've found a natural feeding area, even a single hookbait may well incite a mistake from a feeding carp. We'll look in more detail at bait application later on.

So, what is it that makes a natural feeding zone for the lake's carp? Well, that is hard to specify, as so much depends on the type of lake, its water quality, richness and productivity, the nature of the bottom, weed growth and, of course, the presence of silt deposits and other natural food producing conditions. It figures that the lakes with a controlled head of fish in a rich, highly productive environment, will produce the biggest fish, whilst the overstocked waters with poor quality and little natural food for which the fish are in constant competition, will not push up anything special. You only have to look at the rich gravel pits of the Home Counties to see what I mean.

But gravel pits are not the only lakes capable of growing on big fish. The northern meres, such as the Mangrove, have produced some huge fish.

DIAGRAM 4: WAVENEY C LAKE

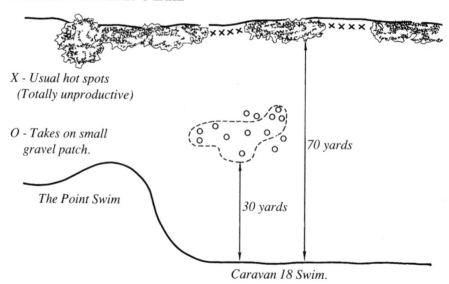

X - Usual hot spots
 (Totally unproductive)

O - Takes on small
 gravel patch.

70 yards

The Point Swim

30 yards

Caravan 18 Swim.

Ken's plan of 'C' lake at Waveney where a change of tactics scored. 'C' lake is pictured on the opposite page.

Waveney 'C' lake.

Indeed, the largest 'known' carp in the U.K. doesn't inhabit some rich southern gravel pit. No, it lives in a northern mere.

Other lakes, such as old sand pits will also produce big carp providing there is enough soft silt and mud to harbour sufficient natural food items. Many of the lakes in northern France are old sand workings used to produce concrete for the motorway network. I believe Rod Hutchinson's syndicate lake is also a lake of this kind, and it is throwing up record after record as I write.

So here you are, on your own water; you have established its type, now you must find the feeding areas and likely hot spots and that means a detailed survey of the lake bed. You are looking for bars and plateaux, weed beds, gravel patches, humps and bumps and soft silt, depths, shallows, anything that departs from the norm. This survey will take time and effort, but if you are going to get the best from the lake, it must be done. You can save a great deal of time and effort by using an echo sounder with 'grey line' facility, but there aren't many clubs who will allow you to do this. As the operation obviously has to be carried out from a boat - and the same clubs probably ban these too, the most efficient method of plotting a lake is a non starter for most of us. I'm afraid all that leaves is the most tedious job in fishing (as far as I'm concerned), that of plumbing and bottom feeling (sounds good doesn't it!).

Enough has been written in other books and articles on this subject, so I'll just deal briefly with it here. The best way to find the depth of a lake is to cast out, using a very buoyant float on the end of the line, which runs through the eye of a heavy bomb. There are many on the market that will serve the purpose. Indeed, there are some so called feature finder floats specially made just for this. Alternatively, you can use a pike float or a swivel bottomed carp float controller, such as those from the Kevin Nash stable (see diagram 5).

It is a straight forward task thereafter, to cast out and reel the buoyant float down until you feel the lead. Open the bail arm and allow the float to rise to the surface, noting the amount of line paid off the reel as you are doing so. Some anglers paint little marks on the rod butt at one and two foot intervals which permits greater accuracy in assessing the depth. Alternatively, simple count the seconds it takes for the float to rise to the surface. Reel the float back down the lead, pull the lead in a few yards and repeat the process right the way back to the margins. In this way you will be able to build up a mental picture of the contours of the bottom. You may want to keep a written record of your findings (diagram 6).

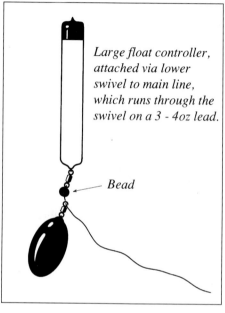

Large float controller, attached via lower swivel to main line, which runs through the swivel on a 3 - 4oz lead.

Bead

DIAGRAM 6

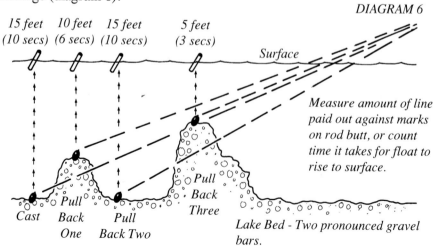

15 feet   10 feet   15 feet   5 feet
(10 secs) (6 secs) (10 secs)   (3 secs)

Surface

Measure amount of line paid out against marks on rod butt, or count time it takes for float to rise to surface.

Pull Back Three

Cast   Back One   Pull Back Two   Pull

Lake Bed - Two pronounced gravel bars.

To assess the nature of the lake bed, take the float off and simply attach the heaviest lead your rod can handle comfortably. You can now cast out as before, but this time you are going to drag the lead back across the bottom, trying to get a feel of the lake bed. Only experience will allow you to interpret the pulls, jerks and bangs felt on the rod tip, but generally speaking, this is what they mean:

1. Lead very hard to pull back after sinking = soft silt or mud.
2. Occasional light resistance; slight jerks = mud bank, weed, silt.
3. Heavier, continuous knocks and rattles of rod tip = gravel patch or hard packed mud or sand ripples.
4. Severe jerks and near solid resistance; lead comes back gouged and damaged = gravel bar or plateau. Presence of mussels.
5. Series of above No. 4 then the line goes slack for a second = a sharp drop off, or steep sided bar. Lead has fallen off top of bar etc.
6. Lead won't come back = snagged up in gravel or rocks, big stones. (This happens frustratingly often!).
7. Lead apparently snagged but comes free after much effort = possibly thick weed bed. Strands or clumps may come in with the lead.

Having charted the bottom, you must now decide what it all means and try to assess each swim accordingly. Not all lakes have bars and plateaux, some have clean, flat bottoms with few or no discernible features and just a thin covering of silt. I have fished many French lakes exactly like this, and finding the fish can be a real headache. In fact, it can be easier finding them on gravel pits and silty meres where problems are posed by gravel bars etc., and areas of deep silt. We'll deal with these in the individual sections looking at the different types of lake.

So now the type of lake is known and the lake bed features and natural feeding areas highlighted. Only now can the angler start to consider the fish themselves and his actual strategy for tackling them.

By now you'll have probably discovered if the fish move with a breeze; if they show themselves to any great extent; if they are loners or go around mob handed and many other patterns of behaviour. Now you must find out about their feeding habits and how much pressure the fish have been under. Are they rig shy? Do they spook from the splash of free offerings? These are some of the things you need to know and there is no better way to find out than by asking questions, and through simple observation.

Provided the questioning isn't **too** blatant - the "gissa bait, gissa rig, show me where to cast" syndrome - the majority of carp anglers will find time to help you out. In fact, first hand experience, provided it isn't too full of 'blinds', will enable you to cut out much of the hard graft you'd normally have to face.

Thereafter if is just a matter of using your eyes. Patterns soon reveal themselves once a few trips are under your belt. Who's catching what and where? Is everyone using one particular approach, and if so, is this because they don't know any better, or is it simply the most effective going method on the fishery at the moment? You can learn a hell of a lot by watching and talking to other well-established anglers.

The final part of any tactical plan has to be bait, and while I shall talk about bait application when I take a more specific look at the tactical approach to various types of water, I don't want to get too involved with bait formulation, or the technical nuts and bolts of the bait world. Mind you, it is hard for me to write in general terms about bait as I am not keen on many of the more popular particles and I don't like using inferior baits.

So, when I come to deal with bait later on, I shall be talking about good quality, balanced nutritional boiled baits, and small mass baits such as dari seed, hemp and groats. I have to admit that I have used some of the larger particles like maples and black eyed beans from time to time and I reluctantly doff my cap to the effectiveness of tiger nuts. I say 'reluctantly' for I firmly believe that they can be harmful to carp (though they are not in the same league of fish killers as the deadly peanut, which should be banned from all carp waters). The size and quality of the bait is something that has to be assessed beforehand, as does flavour and flavour level, other attractors or stimulants, colour and texture. Tim Paisley and Bill Cottam will be writing the bait book of this series and I'll leave the facts, figures and technicalities of the subject to them.

When I first joined Savay, I had my own fixed (possibly too fixed) ideas on bait and I suffered for being too dogmatic, so I was interested in other member's thoughts on bait application for the lake. As so often happens, no two anglers thought the same, but I have always remembered Dave Campbell words of wisdom. Dave is a highly experienced and respected catcher of big fish from Savay and talking to him one day about bait (I know he **always** uses high quality milk protein baits) I was surprised to hear him say that he seldom brought more than one mix with him for a weekend's fishing. He was so confident in the acceptability of his bait and **his pin-point knowledge of the lake bed and feeding areas** that he never felt the need to empty vast quantities of bait into the lake.

"I'd rather have **one** bait in the **right** place than a **thousand** in the **wrong** one", he told me.

Wise words indeed; they certainly made me think twice. I have often fallen into the 'fill it in with bait' trap myself, and while I know I caught many of my better fish on bait quality and strength, I had never considered that I might be working against myself by overbaiting, or excessive baiting in the wrong place. There are too many mistakes mistakes made by anglers filling in the lake

A margin fish caught less than a yard off the bank on Bread Flake.
The angler is Tony Chipman.

with what is a perfectly good bait in all the wrong places. Result - no takes and loss of confidence in the bait. I've been annoyed with otherwise knowledgeable and sensible anglers down here in Cornwall who have consulted me about bait, walked away with a proven fish catching recipe and then thrown their chances of success on it right out of the window through incorrect application.

I guess what I am saying is that it's no good relying totally on a good bait if it's not properly applied to the water you are fishing. As each new lake poses its tactical questions, so bait application needs to figure in the scheme of things in the same way as all the other tactical considerations.

LONG RANGE FISHING

I've already covered the nuts and bolts of long range fishing in the Tackle section, so without going over too much old ground, here are the very basics you will need before you can cast true long distances, by which I mean well over 100 yards.

The rods will obviously need plenty of beef and should be capable of throwing at least a three ounce lead. The rods need to be matched to your own physical strength and stature, but shouldn't be less than a 12' 2.5lb test curve. My own preference is for fast or very fast taper rods. As I mentioned earlier, I don't think the multi range compounds can match true fast taper blanks, and any drawbacks these tippy rods may have as fish playing tools are outweighed by their superior casting abilities. Remember, you are after every inch you can get. Worry about the way the rod handles a fish after you've got one pulling back. My own distance rods are Century's Horizons.

The reel must be either a proper tournament reel or a purpose-designed distance casting one. These models feature a long tapered spool, usually with a two speed crosslay line distribution system to stop the line bedding down on top of itself during retrieve. The Shimano Aero GT Baitrunner 4000 and 4500 models are excellent, as are the range of Daiwa Tournament casting reels such as the new SS 3000. Mind you, at £150 each you'll need a sympathetic missus or bank manager, or maybe you're the lucky sort who doesn't worry about money!

None of these reels look pretty; at first glance they look heavy and cumbersome, but once you have familiarised yourself with their long casting abilities, I think you'll agree that looks aren't everything. My own distance reels are Shimano Biomaster 4000's.

Choice of line is one that has even the experts arguing. There are two schools of thought on the matter. One says that a springy line, such as Sylcast, is best for distance casting as it tends to spring off the face of the reel and achieves extra distance. Others claim that limper lines such as Maxima are better. I have used both makes and can't tell the difference in the casting properties of the two. In fact, I am presently using Golden Marlin 6lbs test nylon and cannot fault it.

I believe choice and breaking strain of the shock leader line is more important. Where snags, bars and other underwater abrasive obstructions are present I'd choose the Berkley Big Game line, marketed by Terry Eustace, whilst for smooth bottomed, silty lakes, I'd go for either Maxima or Golden

23lb 6oz, caught at extreme range, of over 140 yards. Until you see someone carp fishing successfully at this sort of range you don't think it's possible.

Marlin. As a rule of thumb, you'll need a shock leader with a breaking strain five times the number on the lead. In other words, a three ounce lead needs a 15lbs test shock leader; a four ounce lead needs a 20lbs test one and so on.

That is basically all you need (did he say **ALL**???) to set yourself up for distance work. Remember, when you are fishing at range there is a hell of a lot of stretch in the line between the rod tip and the lead. Light indicators may not even register a take at 100 yards plus, so use the heaviest indicators you can get away with. Don't be put off by 25 or even 50 gram monkeys, as they're what you'll need to show cautious pick ups at distance. Choose the heaviest lead that your rod will throw effectively. This isn't just for maximum distance, but to give you something to pull back against when clipping up or adjusting your Baitrunner tension. I like to have the line absolutely bar taut if possible, and you cannot get the line under that sort of tension using two ounce leads.

I suppose more words are written about the mechanics of long range fishing than any other method. After all, many of the biggest carp living in UK waters are often found in massive pits and meres and casts in excess of 100 yards are needed to reach the fish. Of course, this also means that the successful long distance carper needs to be able to get groundbait and free offerings out there as well. I have been fishing two very large waters for some time now and I know just how vital it is to reach some of the distant hot spots in order to stand any chance of a take. For instance, the Gap swim at College may be one that is known to some of you who have fished down in my part of the world during the close season. When the levels are right up, the cast is a good 150 yards off the bank, and at least 125 with the chest waders on. You don't have to be tight to the island trees, but it helps.

The North Bay College Reservoir in Cornwall. Pressure on the fish made long range fishing a necessity at times.

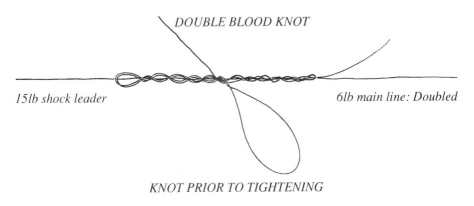

DOUBLE BLOOD KNOT

15lb shock leader   *6lb main line: Doubled*

KNOT PRIOR TO TIGHTENING

AFTER LUBRICATING (use saliva) & TIGHTENING

When I first started fishing College, I found I could catch fish at any range in just about any swim, but as the pressure has built up on the water, the fish have found areas where they know they can get away from some of the pressure - or so they thought. Last year I decided to go back onto College for a few winter trips. Friends had told me that the fish were holed up in the swims by the gap in the island, so I had to re-think my approach.

The 2.5lb 12' Horizons are man enough to throw a three ounce lead a long way and the Shimano Biomasters are certainly the best long distance reels I have used, so I loaded them up with new 6lb breaking strain Golden Marlin and tied in a 36 foot shock leader of 15lb Maxima. By the way, this is the minimum length shock leader I will use - sometimes it's as long as 50 feet. I think that to many anglers the length of the shock leader is always going to be looked upon as something of a compromise. Obviously, in an ideal world you want to get away with the shortest length of heavy line as possible for maximum distance. On the other hand, I have to say that I don't feel happy during a prolonged scrap until I hear the click, click, click of the leader knot passing through the rings and onto the reel. Then the extra leader length comes into its own as the full power of the 15lb test leader and hooklink can now be brought to bear upon the hopefully tiring fish. The knot I use for all joins in two widely varying breaking strain nylons is the Double Blood Knot which is shown in the diagram and is as reliable as anything I've ever needed to use.

The last thing you want flooding through your mind when you have just made a magic cast of a lifetime to a spot never before reached, tight under the overhanging trees 150 yards away, is "I wonder if it's tangled?" It is easy to listen to the nagging voices casting doubts in your mind, so if you're not 100%

confident in your rig as far as tangles are concerned, you'll have some nervy moments wondering if you should check it out after the first runless hour. The 'is it, isn't it' syndrome is a very twitchy one! For most of my fishing at short to medium range, where distance isn't the prime requirement, I'll happily use a stringer and feather the cast as it approaches touch down on the water. This usually prevents tangles and alleviates the use of tubing. However, when I can't afford the slightest impediment to getting the last inch of distance, I use the rig as shown.

The tubing, combined with the Helicopter set-up is

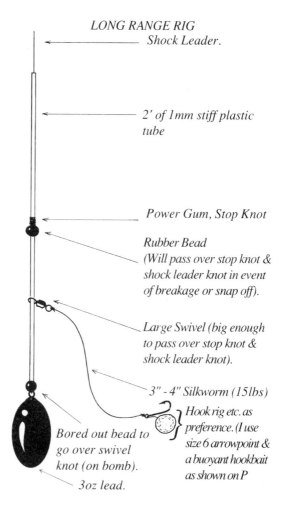

LONG RANGE RIG

Shock Leader.

2' of 1mm stiff plastic tube

Power Gum, Stop Knot

Rubber Bead (Will pass over stop knot & shock leader knot in event of breakage or snap off).

Large Swivel (big enough to pass over stop knot & shock leader knot).

3" - 4" Silkworm (15lbs)

Hook rig etc. as preference. (I use size 6 arrowpoint & a buoyant hookbait as shown on P

Bored out bead to go over swivel knot (on bomb).

3oz lead.

virtually tangle proof, and can be allowed to crash in without feathering or pulling back to straighten the hooklink. The set up is more or less self-explanatory, being a simple adaptation of the silt rig incorporating a heavier, thicker tubing. The top bead is a rubber one that will pass over the stop and shock leader knots, so ensuring that the rig doesn't turn into a Death rig in the event of a snap off. (See the section on Death Rigs towards the end of the book). You'll notice that the hooklink is kept as short as possible. The shorter the hooklink, the further it will cast. Of course, this has to be balanced against the possibility that short hook lengths may have a detrimental effect on the number of pick ups that are converted into fish on the bank, which is why I use the rig as shown as it is ideally suited to hooklinks of no more than 3-4 inches.

So, having sorted out the tackle needed to reach the far margins, I now had to think about getting some free offerings out there. I am not one of those who likes to fish single hook baits unless I'm on one of those waters where the fish have become cautious of big carpets of free offerings. Wherever possible, I like to get a good carpet of freebies laid down in the belief that the harder a carp is feeding on my bait, the easier it will be to catch. Nor can I see the point of laying down a carpet and then casting 20-30 yards past the free offerings just for the sake of it. If I lay down a larder, then I want to fish **on** those freebies, not yards past them. So the ability to bait up at long range is just as important as the ability to cast well.

Baiting up at extreme range used to pose a few problems in the days of catapults and straight throwing sticks. Even the Barnet Diablo or the less effective Black Widow 'pults will be hard pushed to put baits out past the ton and the wear and tear on the elastics will keep you poor! Thankfully the Jumbo Cobra throwing stick has now come to the aid of long range carp fishers.

Baiting up with the Cobra Throwing Stick

Though the Cobra comes in three sizes, I find the Jumbo model is the best one, due to its extra weight. Using the Jumbo Cobra, I now have no trouble in getting large boilies well over the 100 yard mark. In fact, I have measured a throw on dry land using a 22mm bait at 140 yards. Of course, baiting up at this range calls for a hell of a lot of effort and arm strain. You may think that this is taking things to extremes, but I always do a few arm warm-up exercises before getting to work with the Cobra. It definitely saves on torn arm and shoulder muscles!

Of course, the size of the free offerings will dictate just how far you can throw them - up to a point. I have found that my bait goes furthest when rolled to about 22mm. Smaller or larger and they seem to drop a bit short. I take a lot of trouble when making my baits to ensure they are as near perfectly round as I can get them, as this also helps gain those extra yards. If you are using fish meal or bird food bases, you may find that the baits have a tendency to split soon after leaving the barrel. The addition of one or two ounces of egg albumin, or Nutragel, will toughen up the bait during boiling and may help eliminate this tendency. Damping the Cobra and/or the baits will also cut down on the number of splitting baits, but this does tend to reduce distance. Milk protein HNV's seem far less prone to splitting than other types of bait and this must be due to the fact that they are made up with much finer ingredients. Of course, the actual bulk of the base mix is also a vital factor. A bait comprising say, 50% casein will make a heavier 20mm boilie than one containing 50% caseinates.

I should mention the latest gimmick on the market, namely the compressed air powered Boilie Launcher. I have to say that I have not used one, nor even seen one in use, so I cannot comment on their efficiency.

I have found that some of the currently popular bulk oils when used as a post-boiling soak, affect the efficiency of the Cobra by laying down a coating of oil inside the barrel. Some of the oils just get stickier and stickier and are very hard to wash off. In particular, Premier's Nodd Oil and Nutrabaits' Edible Linseed Oil seem particularly hard to shift. I clean the bore of my Cobra regularly, using hot water and plenty of Fairy Liquid, together with a spiral wire tube cleaning brush that you can buy from home brewing shops. Then I polish the accessible inner part of the tube with a silicone furniture polish. Incidentally, I also polish the butt section of the Horizons and the lip of the Biomaster spool. These little touches may seem like unnecessary attention to detail, but when those last few yards are the ones that count, I want to be the guy who's getting there while the others are falling short.

So, the traps were laid and the bait started going in. Over the course of the first few trips to College, I soon realised just how vital it was to get right across tight to the island. At the best of times, with a following wind or, better still, no breeze at all, the cast is just possible, but with any sort of head wind I found

I was falling about ten yards short. Those ten yards were often the difference between success and failure, but over the course of the next few trips I managed to catch enough good carp to satisfy myself that the long range tactics were the most effective ones on the lake **at the time.**

I've stressed those last three words to emphasise a point. No matter how expert one might be at distance casting, I feel it is a fact that the further away from the bank you fish, the less efficiently you do so. I have seen anglers casting prodigious distances, while failing to realise that they are overcasting most of the fish. There is no reason I can see for casting 140 yards when they can be caught at half that distance, so really this is just a warning to keep an open mind about the need to cast vast distances. Sure, it might be necessary and may even be the vital factor, but it shouldn't become a way of life!

Ken James returning a nice mirror caught under the rod tips.

SMALL PITS AND LAKES

Small is a comparative word. In France, they think 100 acres is small! Over here, I suppose most of us consider lakes of 5 acres or less in that category. But just because the water is small, it doesn't follow that the fish will be too. Redmire, Salamander Lake, Darenth Tip, Longfield, some of the Waveney Valley pools, Birch Grove. I'm sure you must have your own qualifiers; all small waters that have produced some outstanding carp.

Speaking for myself, I think small is beautiful. Many of the lakes I fish here in the south west are around the 5 acre mark and I love the intimacy of small, shallow waters where the fish can often be spotted in the margins, stalked on the top or bottom, or simply watched for hours on end, purely for the fun of it. I cut my teeth on such lakes and I think it is true to say that I have learnt more from observing the behaviour of carp in small pools for a few hours than I ever could from weeks and weeks of actually fishing with a bait out there in the wild blue yonder, not knowing what was going on at the business end.

So, imagine a small water of about three acres; a busy park water with lots of bankside disturbance from dog walkers and pram pushers, screaming kids and general hooligans! Sounds lovely doesn't it! - but there are big carp to be caught in there and that makes it all worthwhile. The lake is roughly bean shaped, as if it once followed the contours of a now lost river through low hills. There is a small dam at one end and a stream carrying cool, clear hill run-off water enters at the other end.

Over the years the lake has silted up badly, particularly at the stream entrance where the lack of a natural silt trap has meant that deposits from the winter gales have restricted the inlet end of the pool to less than twelve inches deep. For the rest of the lake, nowhere will you find water more than three feet deep. There seems to be no other distortions of an otherwise smooth bottom, but a 2-3 feet thick layer of silt covers more than 75% of the bottom.

In summer there is prolific weed growth of pondweeds and milfoils. The run-off water always enters the stream a few degrees warmer than the lake water in winter, and a few cooler in summer, while the pH in summer appears steady at 7.8. There are weeping willows all around the lake with the odd ash tree here and there. Over the years, many trees have collapsed into the water, forming pretty awesome snag areas (see diagram 7).

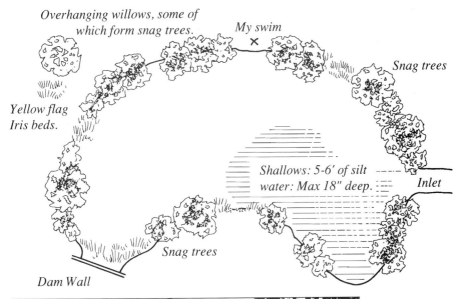

Overhanging willows, some of which form snag trees.

My swim
×

Snag trees

Yellow flag Iris beds.

Shallows: 5-6' of silt water: Max 18" deep.

Inlet

Snag trees

Dam Wall

Stalking

There are few fish in the pond, except a small shoal of roach, the odd perch, lots of eels and, of course, carp, of which there is a mixed head of about thirty fish from low doubles to upper twenties. They have been pressured for more than eight years now and know most of the tricks. A friend of mine once commented, "Never mind that they know every trick in the book; I think they wrote the bloody thing!"

Coming onto the water for the first time posed new problems for me. Mind you, locating the fish wasn't one of them, for you could often see them in the summer months when the water was gin clear and the fish were clearly visible as they basked in the sun or fed, heads down in the silt. Indeed, finding the areas of natural food wasn't a problem either; the silt was alive with food and they could get a feed wherever they stuck their heads down and they betrayed their feeding activity by sending up vast clouds of disturbed silt and mud to discolour the water. So, in fact, my only (what do you mean, **only**!) problems centred around the fish themselves. This is often the case on small waters, as patrol routes and feeding stages soon become apparent, thus allowing one to centre one's thoughts on the nitty-gritty of it all - the fish.

I found the lads on the water helpful, but not optimistic about my chances. These fish made very few mistakes they told me and they don't particularly need to eat baits; there's so much natural food. All the particles have been tried and while milk based HNV's had worked for a long time on the lake, they had apparently stopped working a few years ago. Patrol routes? No particular pattern. In summer, the fish lie up on the surface at the inlet and in all the snags and they seem to feed at night. In winter, they feed for about an hour around midday - but not every day, and not always in the same place. They follow warm winds in summer but apparently not in winter. They are spooky of bait carpets, flavours and rigs and prebaiting is a no-no due to water foul and eels.

What else? Well, for one thing they are aware of anglers - very much so. If you are walking around and you spot a fish in the water, try not to stop dead and look at it. They will tolerate moving bankside disturbance, but they bolt from stationary ones. They seem to know anglers can't fish on the run! In all but the very coldest of weather, the fish certainly cover every inch of the bottom during a 24 hour period. Certainly they will encounter and move over your baits many times over the course of a session. If you aren't getting takes, there's something wrong with your bait and/or your rig. Too many anglers is the kiss of death and tight lines similar - anything else you want to know? Yes - where's another pool????!

First consideration, a bait. From what I'd learnt, the majority of the anglers on the pool were on particles still, with tiger nuts being in favour at the time. One guy was catching more than his share - friend Steve was consistently catching on ready mades but he wasn't giving too much away apart from that. O.K., I figured that if they were happy with shop boilies it could be that they would react favourably to a reintroduction of milk HNV's. Spooky of boilies/colours/flavours? Try an alternative attractor; try to match the colour to the lake bed; make them a different shape and texture.

I went for a cubed jelly based milk/birdfood HNV with an essential oil attractor at a very low level. That changed all the bait parameters. Now to see if they like it. The best place to test baits on any water is in the snags. In the safety of the tangled branches, the fish feel far more confident about picking up suspicious foodstuffs that they might well ignore in open water.

So, one bright summer morning, there I was in the trendy camouflage gear, pretending to be part of a tree while just below me, not five feet away, half a dozen big fish swam hesitantly over a carpet of my chosen offerings. They were a bit nervous at first, but I suspect this was simply because the foodstuff itself was obviously foreign and unnatural. I couldn't believe that the jelly/oil approach had been used before - but you never can tell. So it was with great relief that I watched as the fish began feeding hesitantly on the bait. Within an hour they had disposed of 400 baits - seems they like it!

Next consideration, an effective terminal set up. Catching carp is all about being versatile. I looked at the choices and the problems. There was no need to cast a great distance. In fact, the best chances would be most likely to fall to margin fished baits during darkness. I'd hazard a guess that everyone on the lake was on the usual anti-eject, heavy lead bolt rig. I remembered a trip we'd had to a new water where Carole had action on very long hooklinks and comparatively light half ounce bombs, and wondered it anyone had tried anything as silly here. Could be worth a try.

A few years ago, long Dacron hooklinks had been all the rage, admittedly with heavy bombs, but I could mess around with ledger weights until I got it right. So, after much pondering under the thinking cap I felt a long confidence rig would score, particularly with the soft baits which they might crush in their lips rather than throwing them right back to the throat teeth.

I plumped for a combination link of about four feet with three feet of 15lb Silkworm water knotted to a foot of Kryston Multistrand; hook a size 6 barbless Partridge Arrowpoint with a tiny ring tied in at the hook knot. (See diagram 8). The hookbait, a buoyant boilie, using the same attractors as the free jelly based offerings, would be tied to the ring with dental floss and counterbalanced so as to fish right on the bottom without sinking into the silt.

Most of the swims are quite tight and overgrown with the marginal willows jutting out on either side. Twelve footers would be needed to keep out beyond the trees whilst playing a fish. The Simpson's KM2's would do fine with the 55's and 15lb main line; a bit heavy I know, but don't forget all the snags and the prolific weed.

As for the bankside set up, this too would need to be well thought out. The bivvy would need to be set up well back from the lake - can't risk light or noise

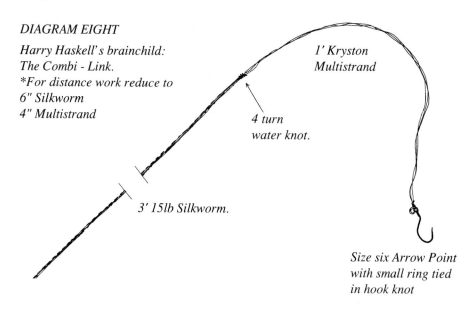

DIAGRAM EIGHT

Harry Haskell's brainchild:
The Combi - Link.
**For distance work reduce to*
6" Silkworm
4" Multistrand

1' Kryston
Multistrand

4 turn
water knot.

3' 15lb Silkworm.

Size six Arrow Point
with small ring tied
in hook knot

if they are that aware. I would be expecting most of the action after dark when they might feel more confident and the bankside disturbance had died down. Rods must be set well back, not overhanging the water, risking shadows. Margin leads an absolute necessity (I use the clip on Gardner type) to keep the line anchored to the bottom. Remember what the lads had said about tightly clipped up lines? (See diagram 9).

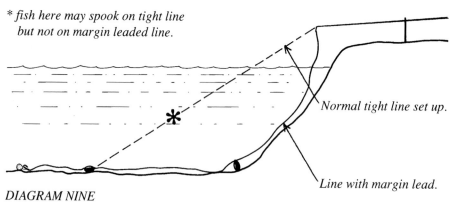

* fish here may spook on tight line
* but not on margin leaded line.*

Normal tight line set up.

Line with margin lead.

DIAGRAM NINE

Showing how the clip-on margin lead holds the line tight
to the bottom thus avoiding spooking fish.

I would be using stringers, not traditional lengths tied to the hook, but a loop of free offerings tied around the hookbait. (See diagram 10). This has worked for me so often when the carp are playing hard to get that I'm surprised I've never seen anybody else using it. The 200 or so free offerings were tied up using PVA thread into small clumps of ten or a dozen baits and thrown in an arc pattern around the swim. This would hopefully pull down fish approaching the swim from any direction. The idea of the clumps of bait is fairly obvious. Once the fish got used to finding and feeding on these tight clumps of bait, their somewhat tunnelled vision of artificial baits would be overcome and they would feed confidently, even when they came to the clump with the hookbaits in them. (See diagram 11 on page 78).

DIAGRAM TEN

Normal Stringer   — *Hookbait*

Baits tied to bend with PVA strip.

Looped Stringer   *Hookbait*

Baits tied around hookbait to form a loop: tie either from eye or bend of hook.

That's the plan. Did it work? Would I be telling you all this if it didn't! I had some very special results on the pool, taking most of the better fish in there. It has to be said that Steve continued to catch on his ready mades, but I discovered later that he was being very crafty in the amount of bait he fed and the terminal rig he was using. By keeping free offerings to a minimum with cooked pop-ups critically balanced on a form of bent hook rig, he was picking up fish that were still suspicious, but thought they could get around the standard set ups that the other anglers were using. Bait application and much thought on terminal tackle brought him his rewards.

DIAGRAM ELEVEN

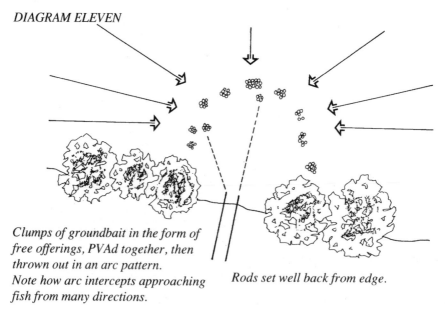

Clumps of groundbait in the form of free offerings, PVAd together, then thrown out in an arc pattern. Note how arc intercepts approaching fish from many directions.

Rods set well back from edge.

I fished the pool, on and off, for another couple of years. The fish got wise to my bait and tactics quite soon, but it wasn't too hard to keep one step ahead of them. That's the beauty of small waters, you can watch the carp's reaction to changes in bait and presentation and see if they're working or not. For instance, in my last season on the water, I wanted to try an almost revolutionary (by today's thinking) approach. I started fishing amino acid paste baits, freelined in the margins, using about 4 feet of Multistrand water-knotted to the end of the reel line. A small, light hook (Hilton size 10) was then tied on to the Multistrand and buried in a small knob of soft paste. No bomb, no hair - right back to Walker's day. A light scattering of free paste offerings brought the fish down onto the baits and when they picked up the hookbait they didn't seem to even know they'd got it. That tactic brought me a string of good fish, and even though I showed some of the other lads what I was doing, they must have thought I was winding them up, so they took no notice and continued blanking.

All of the above happened on a lake I no longer fish. It is, if you like, a compendium of my experiences on it over the years, but I hope it serves to illustrate the pain and pleasure of difficult, small water carping.

Anglers have since come and gone on the lake - most have departed sadder and wiser men. The carp in there can be among the most frustrating creatures I know. I have watched them swim backwards and forwards over a carpet of bait for hours on end, totally ignoring it, yet apparently not worried at all by its presence. Other times they'll bow wave and top over the bait without a sign of a take, and sometimes they'll flee in fright at the very sight of a single bait. What are they reacting to? If I knew that I'd catch a lot more!

Of course, odd fish do get caught from time to time, but it is no coincidence that the anglers with their thinking caps on are the most successful. When you are faced with a similar set of circumstances, remember that carp have a brain the size of a pea. They aren't MENSA candidates, no matter how frustrating they may at first appear. Small water carp are a challenge because they are right there at the sharp end. You can watch them and see their reactions to various angling situations.

Sometimes they can drive you potty, then it's back to the drawing board time. Hopefully you'll get it right next time!

A useful small water ploy. A variation on the stringer theme.

LARGE LAKES AND RESERVOIRS

I'll expect you'll have your own ideas on what qualifies a water as 'big'. I remember when I first saw College, I thought it was absolutely immense, but that was because I'd previously only fished small lakes. At the time, forty acres was daunting, but having since fished waters ten times bigger, College now seems like a puddle. So it's all comparative. One man's ocean is another's little pool.

Some of the European waters just blow your mind. The first thought is "How am I going to even begin tackling a water this size? Where are the fish going to be?"

Remember what I said before? First find the food larders? It's no different on big waters. Of course, the bigger a lake, the harder it may be to find feeding areas. However, it isn't impossible by any means and work done in preparation will never be wasted. Here's an example.

The northern French lake was very big; perhaps 250 acres. We'd never fished it before, never even clapped eyes on it before and it looked awesome. Oddly shaped, with two arms running east to west, one off each long bank. It was an old flooded sand working, a small river having been dammed to allow the shallow basin to fill. When full, the average depth would have been about 12 feet, but after a long summer drought the water was well down and the depth had been reduced to no more than about 8 feet. The lake bed was more or less flat, with few mounds, bars or depressions to act as food traps. Yet there was obviously plenty of food in there if the size of the carp was anything to go by. The water quality looked good with slightly coloured water and a rough pH of 8.0.

A slow stroll around the lake took over three hours. Time well spent, for we saw enough encouraging signs to make the prospect of fishing this bare looking expanse of water a little less daunting. There were odd swan mussel shells washed up in the margins and a plentiful hatch of insect life indicated the richness of the water. Best of all were the occasional heavy splashes as good sized carp showed off in the fresh south westerly breeze. Because the lake hadn't seen all that much angling pressure, it followed that without large quantities of bait, the fish had to have grown to such a size on a diet of natural food - so go find it.

On lakes of this size, a boat is absolutely essential and even if, like us, you can only afford a kid's little plastic dinghy, it's better than nothing. A quick row around with a sounding pole showed a perfectly flat lake bed and an even depth of 8 feet. We could find little evidence of any weed beds, but there surely had to be areas of natural food to be found. Here and there, as we prodded the bottom with the pole, instead of meeting fairly solid resistance from the hard sand bottom, it would sink several inches into soft silt. The end of the pole was thick with bloodworm rich mud and silt. Surely an obvious larder that would be visited by all the lake's cyprinids at one time or another.

I put a big marker float on the original soft patch and then groped my way around with the sounding pole, gradually expanding the silt patch, eventually finding it to be almost circular in pattern and some 60 yards in diameter. How about that for a carp restaurant! It was hard graft, faffing about in the silly little dinghy, but it was worth every minute. The silt patch was well within casting range and once we'd marked the lines with small dental floss tags and taken sighting marks off the far bank trees, we brought in the big marker float out of the way.

I felt sure the silt would be the hot spot and gambled on a big heap of strongly flavoured particles, groats and boiled baits, to pull the fish down. It isn't a tactic I'd like to employ in the U.K., but I'd learnt from previous trips that most French fish haven't become so wary of commercial flavours as their English counterparts. Sure enough, the fish responded to our baits very well and we were rewarded with almost non-stop action over the course of the five day trip. Nothing huge was caught, but we had great fun with the very pretty double figure carp that flocked to the bait carpet.

That's all very well, you might say, but what about the harder English waters? Point taken, but I think the lesson from the French example must be that we probably wouldn't have caught anything like so many fish if we hadn't first established the whereabouts of the natural food, before having the guts to pile plenty of bait in to try and wean them off the naturals and on to our offerings.

By comparison, let's look at another example; this time an English water. The lake is a mature, well established reservoir of about 42 acres. Surrounded by thick woods, nestling in a slight valley, it has been formed on a flooded river plain. Just by looking at the gently sloping surroundings, you can tell that it probably isn't going to be deep, and later plumbing reveals a fairly uniform bottom some 6-8 feet deep. There should be plenty of silt formed by leaf deposits and other decaying organic matter. A pH reading shows a rather disappointing pH but that should still encourage plenty of natural food, mostly bloodworm, snails, freshwater shrimp and mussels. The prevailing wind is a south westerly which runs more or less straight up the valley along the length of the lake. It would seem likely that fish will move on such a wind,

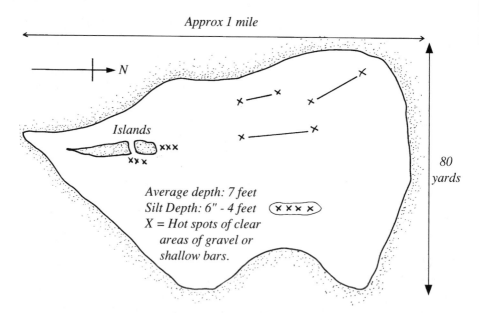

Approx 1 mile

N

Islands

xxx
xyx

80
yards

Average depth: 7 feet
Silt Depth: 6" - 4 feet
X = Hot spots of clear
    areas of gravel or
    shallow bars.

but can you be certain? Remember, not all waters are affected by weather influences. (See diagram 12).

The owner doesn't permit boats, swimming or wading, so the only way to get a feel of the bottom is by casting around and plumbing. This proves to be somewhat tricky, for your earlier guess about silt deposits appears correct, with much of the bottom being covered in thick silt deposits of up to three or four feet deep in places. So profuse is the silt, that it is almost impossible to discern any variable features on the bottom and, eventually, you will rightly conclude that with so much soft stuff on the bottom, the fish will be able to put their heads down and get a feed just about anywhere. But surely they will have areas they prefer? Maybe in the vast beds of water milfoil that show at the surface in the shallows, down at the far end of the lake. Certainly the carp will feed where they feel most secure. In the snags, or around the sole island at the south end of the lake. There is still so much to find out!

Your research has shown a good head of carp. Say 250 doubles and a number of decent twenties. They have been under fairly intense angling pressure for the past ten years and are getting pretty cute, but the carp like their boilies and seem to make fairly regular visits to the bank with a crowd around them. Most baits have seen service over the years, but the fish meals/oils rule the roost at the moment, with plenty of fish falling for the oil drenched baits. So bait choice is more or less settled for you before you even start. It's not like the small pool example where the fish are wary about **all** baits. Here the fish are known to be falling to one particular approach and you'd be silly to deviate from this. Mind you, keep a close eye on things. The longer they keep making mistakes on one particular bait, the more suspicious they will eventually get of it, regardless of the bait's nutritional worth.

The steady pressure over the years has meant that the going swims have become well established. You could become a free spirit and 'boldly go where no man has gone before' but to start off you feel more confident in one of the established swims. It's a fair bet that others before you have tried the Starship Enterprise approach anyway, and that's how the swims have gradually become opened up around the lake. You notice, in fact, that many of the well worn swims, indicating greater use, are at the southern end of the lake. This despite the fact that the prevailing wind should move fish well away from that area. Does that mean that the fish don't follow the breeze?

The entrance to the North Bay at Savay. This area can become a hot spot at the whim of the weather.

You turn your thoughts to presentation. In all that silt it's got to be spot on, but then, is it important to have baits sitting up on the top of the silt? I remember as a very inexperienced big water angler going on to College for the first time, I had no idea what the bottom was like and for the most part, just chucked and chanced. I caught a great many carp on short, four inch bolt rigs and two ounce leads. It was only later that I discovered that the swims I'd been fishing had two feet of soft silt on the bottom. The bait must have been buried from sight under at least a foot of the silt, yet the carp still found them.

Of course, there are waters where correct silt presentation is very important, and the new water may be one of them. You recall the experiences of some friends who have been fishing a big northern mere with silt deposits twenty feet deep in places. The silt rig developed for these northern waters should fit the bill here. It is an adaption of a helicopter rig incorporating a short sliding hook length, allowing the bait to sit up on the top of the silt - in theory. I say, in theory, for I don't believe that you can ever have a terminal arrangement guaranteed 100% successful at keeping your hookbait out of the silt (always accepting that this is necessary). There are simply too many variables to take into account, not the least of which is knowing the exact depth of the silt in the first place. Still, it is a good rig for most silt situations and should get you your share. (See diagram 13).

THE SILT RIG

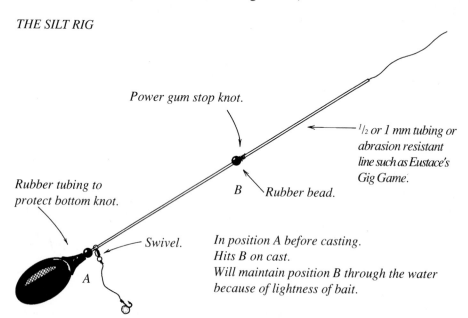

Power gum stop knot.

$^1/_2$ or 1 mm tubing or abrasion resistant line such as Eustace's Gig Game.

Rubber tubing to protect bottom knot.

B   Rubber bead.

Swivel.

In position A before casting.
Hits B on cast.
Will maintain position B through the water because of lightness of bait.

A

Paul Noble with a big reservoir fish caught at 60 yards at a time when most anglers were over-casting the fish.

Having settled on a suitable rig, you now want a bait that won't sink out of sight in seconds in the soft stuff. Or do you? Just how necessary is this? With so much of the lake bed being covered in a layer of thick silt, the carp must be completely used to finding their food buried in the bottom. Why set up a possible area of suspicion by offering brightly coloured food items in full view on top of the silt. You decide to go in with two base mixes. One will be your standard fish meal mix, while the other will substitute some lighter ingredients like Casilan or shrimp meal to make the baits more buoyant. Time will tell which will prove the most effective.

With all the groundwork now completed, it simply remains to see if your tactical plan works. There's no reason why it shouldn't, given that the fish have been located, the lake bed plumbed and charted for areas of natural food. The rig is a proven catcher on similar waters and, finally, the bait is already established. So what do you do if it all goes wrong? And even the best laid plans fall to bits at times.

So imagine that the first five or six trips have not lived up to expectations. It might not necessarily be time for a prolonged session with the drawing board! For instance, ask yourself if your results mirror those of others on the water. If no one else is doing well either, it could well be that the fish are just doing a moody. They might have eventually wised up to the proliferation of fish baits, or a prolonged high pressure hot spell has put them off the feed. On the other hand, suppose it's just you who's suffering. Everybody else on the lake is getting action, so why aren't you?

This is when it pays to be patient. It would be all too easy to change rig/bait/swim all at once and still not catch. For instance you might well have changed a bad rig for a better one, but the bait that you've discarded was a far better one than the replacement. Result - you still don't catch! So logic dictates that you change things slowly - one step at a time. Assuming that the hypothetical situation described above remains the same (i.e. there are still plenty of fish coming out on the fish meals), you think it might be likely that the terminal presentation is wanting in some respect. (I'll take a general look at terminal tackle in the last chapter).

So, you improve your presentation - hopefully! Still action is slow. You feel sure the bait is going and the rig is as good as you can get it, yet you keep on struggling. In our rather simplistic hypothetical world, there can only be one thing left. You haven't done your homework properly. Let's go back to our early recce sessions. You have found the whole of the lake bed to be covered by an overall blanket of silt; so much so that you are unable to discern any other features such as areas of clean gravel or hard packed mud banks rising proud of the mud. Maybe there are small bars or humps that aren't buried under a foot or two of silt. Could it be that the lads who are catching are doing so on these cleaner areas? Or maybe they're fishing the weed beds that you've carefully avoided so far. The reason for your failure isn't due to either bait or rig, both of which may be perfectly acceptable. No, it's simply down to the fact that the others are fishing on the clean areas, while you are in the silt! No doubt the fish have been quite happy eating your hookbaits six inches down in the silt and your silt rig has been effective at catching the silt feeding carp, but all the successful boys are doing is offering the same bait on the same rig, but in a more obvious spot.

Just going back for a minute to that first year on College. It was a year when the water level dropped most dramatically and, at one stage, I guess the reservoir was only half full - if that. As the level dropped, the areas where we'd successfully caught carp all through the winter were exposed. What we'd taken to be a relatively flat, silt covered area was revealed as a series of clean gravel mounds and mud banks with silt filled gullies in between. None of the features was more than 12 inches high, yet they were obviously areas that the fish visited in the course of their feeding activity. No doubt they also visited the silty areas where they found some of our free offerings, but those on the features stood out better and allowed better presentation and perhaps, hook penetration. Once these features were pinpointed, we always tried to find them when casting out. We weren't worried where the freebies went, the fish

Ken with a lovely 20+ common from College Reservoir.

were surely eating them wherever they went, but the hookbaits up on the features always outfished the ones in the silt.

Incidentally, you soon get to recognise the 'feel' of a lead when it drops down into the silt. It's a soft, soggy type of feeling. The clean crisp thud as the lead touches down on the hard bits is what you are looking for.

So, that's a look at bigger waters. If you do your groundwork properly I think you'll find them easier than the hard pressured, small waters. Some popular big lakes may, at first, seem heavily pressured, but I think they can absorb a lot more angling pressure than smaller waters before they can be classed as truly 'hard'. The wind and other weather conditions will probably influence the carp more than on smaller waters, and, nine times out of ten, you won't need the finnicky terminal rigs that may be the difference between success or failure on the ultra hard, small waters.

GRAVEL PITS

Gravel pits come in all shapes and sizes and some contain very big carp. It would be easy to assume from the weekly papers that **all** big carp live in gravel pits; most of them situated in the Colne Valley, Kent and Essex. I suppose there's some validity in that. Savay, Harefield, Harrow and Darenth are just a few waters almost constantly in the news with big thirties, and even forties. All are old gravel workings, with a common denominator in the richness of their water. High pH values, vast natural food stocks and low stock levels contribute to the well being of the carp and the size to which they grow. Anglers' bait helps maintain a steady flow of nutritional (hopefully) artificial foodstuff into the water, so improving the carp's body weight and condition.

Though locating carp on massive pits like Savay or Wraysbury can indeed be a daunting task, once found they are often quite easy to tempt onto baits. However, location is made harder due to the complexity of the underwater terrain and the presence of islands and weedbeds and finding the fish can prove the hardest part. Preparation, in the form of plumbing and assessing the nature of the lake bed is perhaps more critical on pits than on any other type of water. Bars, plateaux, gullies and weed beds will need to be pinpointed, and once found, assessed in terms of their likely food holding potential and how they will respond to changing weather conditions. I've fished quite a few pits of differing sizes and all have responded readily to weather influences, especially the wind. Where bars come close to the surface, the prevailing winds will channel silt, and thus food deposits, to the down wind end of the bar. (See diagram 14). If the bar lies across the direction of the prevailing wind, more silt will be deposited on the lee side of the bar than on the windward side. (See diagram 15).

Converging bars and plateaux will accumulate food as the wind sends currents over and around the feature. Snails and mussels prefer a flow of water across a feature to bring them their food. While shallow features will affect the way the wind carries and deposits food holding silt, there are several differences of opinion among top anglers as to the best places to fish. I know the consensus at Savay is heavily weighted in favour of fishing **off** the silt. I think this is because of the nature of the silt itself, as it is deep and stinking in places. I do know that many of the most successful anglers on the lake have pinpointed soft

DIAGRAM FOURTEEN

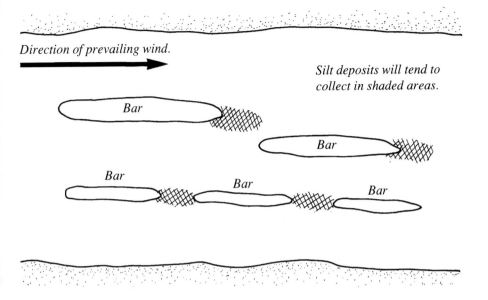

Direction of prevailing wind.

Silt deposits will tend to collect in shaded areas.

DIAGRAM FIFTEEN

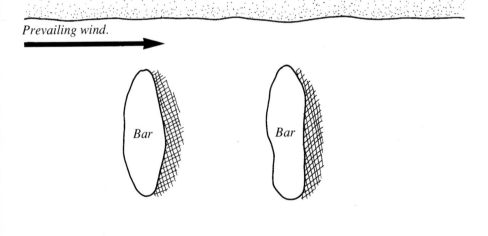

Prevailing wind.

areas that seem to produce good numbers of fish. Perhaps these are areas of sweeter, richer silt. However, for the most part, the general tactic is to pull back after casting until the rod tip shows the beginning of a bar or a patch of cleaner gravel.

On the other hand, one very well known Savayite told me when I joined, "Just chuck out and leave it. They feed everywhere so leave it where it lands!"

He catches a lot of fish so maybe there's a lot in what he says. Maybe we do make life more difficult than it needs to be.

A quick word of warning on uncorroborated advice. I was told in all sincerity by a long standing and much respected member of the syndicate that a particular swim on Savay was "not more than 8 feet deep, with regular bars and very little silt". Last year, while fishing this swim during the drastic heat wave, I cooled down with a swim over much of the area. I found no bars, depths down to ten feet and silt two feet deep in places! Mind you, the guy has had fish to 35lb from the swim, so even getting it as wrong as that hasn't affected his fishing too much!

The next example is of a small 6 acre gravel pit in Norfolk where Carole and I spent several fishing holidays over the past seven years. The lake is more or less square, with a fairly uniform depth of between 8-12 feet. Around some of the edges runs a marginal shelf about three or four feet wide and some two

DIAGRAM SIXTEEN

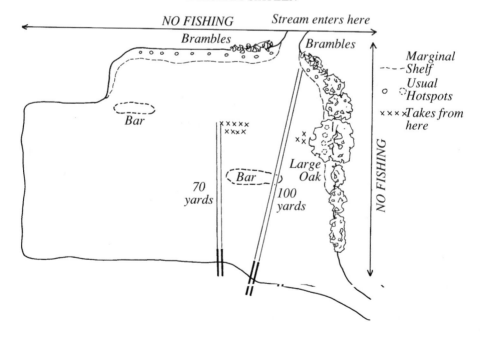

"The fish are wise beyond their years and have seen it all.

feet depth, and it is on these that a great deal of angling attention is focused. The few bars that exist are relatively small features, but are nonetheless important, as the carp pick up baits off them on a regular basis. The pit is well over forty years old with a layer of deep, foul smelling silt over much of its bed, caused by years of accumulated leaf detritus. (See Diagram 16).

The carp population is high. One estimate puts the number at 300, which is a lot for a 6 acre lake. They range from singles to mid thirties and have been subjected to considerable angling pressure for the past fifteen years. The fish are wise beyond their years and have seen it all!

Natural food production is not high, due to the fairly obnoxious nature of the silt, but bloodworm, mussels and shrimp are all there in good quantities. However, the carp have come to rely to a large extent on anglers' baits for a proportion of their everyday food intake, and most of the accepted baits have taken fish over the years. Two banks are unfishable, so there is plenty of sanctuary for the carp. On the other hand, with the right tackle, the long cast to the far bank isn't too difficult and many fish trip up on baits tight to the bank on the marginal shelf.

We went up for a week in the November of 1987. It was our fourth visit and by now we thought we had enough experience and knowledge to ensure we wouldn't have to do too much groundwork. I knew I'd need to cast at least 100 yards across to the far margins, so we took the Horizons for me, while Carole relied on the Spirolites. Reels were Abbu 55's loaded with 6lb line to 15lb shock leaders, to handle the three ounce leads.

The usual hot spots along the far margin were apparently still producing fish, as were the small gravel patches along the right hand margin (also unfishable). I did a bit of plumbing around just to get the feel of things once more and quickly rediscovered the small bar at about fifty yards which had yielded a couple of takes on the last trip, even though it only came up a couple of feet. I felt sure the lake would fish exactly as it had for us in the past. In other words, tight to the back, under the trees on the right hand bank, or on the gravel banks.

Friends who had fished during the summer had given us plenty of advice on bait but the fish have seen so many different flavours, oils, amino acid liquids and other attractors that we wondered what to try next. General consensus was for a milk HNV with a combination of very low level essential oils as attractors. We only had a week on the lake but experience said 'make your choice, believe in it and stick with it to the end'. They sometimes take some time getting onto a bait, but keep it going in little and often, was the message. I was just coming off College at the time and the garlic oil/Richworth Blue Cheese combination had worked a treat down there, so maybe it was worth a try here.

Rigs? Who knows what had been seen on the lake since our last visit. I'd heard that 2-3" pop-ups using small baits tight to the shank of the hook had worked well during the summer, but that the carp had stopped falling for that one as the autumn months drew close. We chose a simple eye-tied hair, using a ten inch multi-stranded nylon hooklink made up with one pound breaking strain Maxima (the forerunner of today's Kryston's Multistrand material and still much used by many experienced anglers in this country). Hook was a Hilton barbless, size 6. We used a small piece of foam as a rig stop, this being just sufficient to keep the hook afloat if no bait was attached. This should have the effect of making the hookbaits behave in like manner to the free offerings. The hair was such that the bend of the hook just cleared the top of the boilie after the stop was in place. Nothing terribly earth shattering there, eh?

The weather couldn't have been better, with warm and wet south westerlies blowing almost all week, conditions, past experience had told us, that the fish respond favourably to. We started putting the bait in at the rate of three pounds of milk HNV 18mm baits per day. This went in under the trees off to the right, in particular under the overhanging oak tree that dominates the right hand bank, and along the far marginal shelf, tight against some bramble bushes where a small stream enters the lake. Full of confidence, it was just a matter of counting the short hours until the first fish made a mistake.

We were still counting 72 hours later, without so much as a run! Help - what was happening here? Carole and I had a committee meeting and decided to try the less favoured areas well away from the (until now) hot spots. I tried coming in from the far margin about 20-25 yards. There was nothing particularly significant in that distance, it just felt right. Sometimes instinct plays a bigger tactical part in carp fishing than anything else! I wondered if the fish had become spooky of the carpets of different baits that must pile up on the marginal shelf right through the summer. Perhaps a carpet of bait these few yards in from the back might trick the carp into making a mistake.

I'd caught on the lake in the past by offering a carpet of baits with one smell, while using a hookbait with a completely different one over the top. I'm sure this entices the take, more out of curiosity than anything else. I stayed with the garlic/cheese combination for the free offerings but switched to small geranium and clove oil hookbaits over the top - and it worked! I had two runs within four hours of the new bait going in on the new area. Carole switched her rods there as well and we ended our week with nine fish and lost three over the last three days. A pleasant reward for imagination and hard work and the confidence to try something different when the accepted tactics aren't working.

Something different...Carole caught this mirror on an 8' dacron hooklink and half ounce bomb.

By contrast, a new gravel pit was a completely unknown quantity. Roughly half a diamond in shape, it was 25 acres of underwater terrain that must have looked like the dark side of the moon! Plumbing had revealed numerous bars, plateaux and gravel mounds, with large beds of pondweed, milfoil and water lilies scattered in profusion about the lake. Three small islands nestled in the northern bay area making it a perfect silt/food trap in the prevailing south westerly winds. The gullies between the islands ran some 8-9 feet deep with a thin layer of fine silt which had accumulated at the narrowest part between two of the islands. (See Diagram 17).

DIAGRAM SEVENTEEN

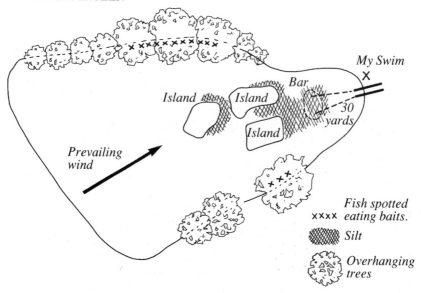

I decided to concentrate my campaign in this spot and spent several hours with a plumbing rod, searching the whole lake bed between and around the two facing islands. The south west wind would surely push carp up towards the islands and it would also funnel through the gap, depositing silt and forming those natural food larders that are so important.

I knew that this work was going to be the most crucially important on this new lake. As far as I knew, it hadn't been fished for a great many years and the carp population was an unknown quantity. So, faced with carp that would be 'green' on both rigs and bait, the most vital aspect of my tactical plan would be the actual location; then simply it would be a question of introducing a plentiful supply of a nutritional food source to establish it as such with the carp.

I spent many hours just wandering the banks, looking for signs of fish, at the same time introducing a couple of pounds of a proven HNV bait at random around the lake. It was noticeable that they seemed to move on the warm south westerlies, judging by the amount of movement I saw up in the northern part of the lake whenever the wind freshened up. Now I wanted to find out if they were on the bait.

I had found a couple of spots where I could actually see if the bait was being eaten. Along part of a willow strewn bank, overhanging branches had shaded the bottom to such an extent that the weed had failed to establish itself. The bottom was clean, bright gravel, about five fee deep, dropping away once clear of the treeline. I started introducing bait at regular intervals and was delighted to note that a pound mix was disappearing overnight, within about a week of the first lot going in, and on one visit I was lucky enough to see the fish actually eating the bait. Nothing huge, but they looked good upper

A typical fat gravel pit fish taken on a fish meal bait.

doubles with a few nice twenties mixed in.

The plumbing had revealed a nice little bar right in front of my chosen swim facing two of the islands. It was only about thirty yards out and came up about three feet to form a nice little plateau some four or five yards across. It looked an ideal spot to pick up fish as they moved with the breeze up between the islands and I decided to start fishing there on the plateau. No distance to cast so I used the Simpson's KM's to cast running two ounce leads and simple Dacron bolt rigs out to the plateau. Using a bait dropper on the Horizon, I laid down a carpet of heavily flavoured groats on the top of the bar along with about a hundred boiled baits. The forecast gave a fresh south westerly and, from what I had seen on my walkabouts, I was expecting a lot of fish to move onto the bait at once, pushed up by the breeze. The trap was set, now it was time for 'sit and wait tactics'.

The wind freshened as it got dark and with it came the first sign of fish on the baits. Nothing dramatic - just quiet head and shouldering; that's a good sign. I think that fish continuously crashing out over the baits means that they are responding to the smell, but in the wrong place. They are trying to feed where the attractor level smells right to them, and this may not necessarily be

Carole with a typical big water French common.

*Ken returns a 20lb
plus common to the
same water.*

on the bait itself. This is a classic example of flavour overload and I feel sure
it explains that often quoted phenomenon where carp are forever crashing out
on top of the baits but none are taken. Head and shouldering, or rolling, is
different and usually indicates that fish are feeding. Runs can be expected at
any time.

It turned out to be a good night. The fish fed hard until about midnight,
when the action slowed. By then, five nice fish had been landed. They were
crammed with groats and I can't help feeling that the reason the runs stopped
is because there wasn't enough bait to hold them. Sometimes it's very hard to
know just how much you'll need, and I suppose it's better to start on the light
side and build up as you go along. Of course, you then run the risk of under-
baiting and by the time you wake up to that fact it's too late and they've moved off.

I hope these examples of how I fished two very different gravel pits may
give you a few ideas to try out on your local waters. I often think that many
anglers are intimidated by gravel pits, be they large or small, but they can be
ridiculously easy to read. Like all waters, time spent doing your groundwork
will pay dividends. It's just a matter of using your eyes and then your head.
Once you've found the fish, the rest gets a lot easier.

OTHER TACTICAL CONSIDERATIONS

I love stalking fish, but I don't really think I can take too much space up describing tactics for stalking. I know this way of fishing leaves many people cold as they think the 3B's approach is the only worthwhile one. O.K. Each to their own.

I also have to accept that on many waters the sheer amount of angling pressure means stalking tactics are out of the question, but for all that, there will still be a few waters where you might be able to stalk margin fish - as much on small waters as on the bigger ones. (Witness Chris Ball's floater results on Wraysbury and the numerous Savay fish that have been stalked off the top in the past few seasons).

I regard every stalking session as another angling lesson. There is so much one can learn simply by watching fish and there's nothing more exciting than seeing a good fish sidling slowly up to your hookbait. Sometimes my heart is going so loud and fast that it feels like it's trying to get out of my body. That's how stalking fish gets to me at times.

I never use buzzers or more than one rod when stalking fish. They're not conducive to efficient stalking anyway. I use two outfits for my stalking sessions. One is a Simpson's stalker butt on the top section of my K.M. 2 Dual Taper. This is matched with an ABU 55, loaded with 15lb line and is used for snag fishing. The open water outfit is usually one of the twelve foot Spirolites, again with a 55, this time loaded with 8lb breaking strain line. I carry a selection of floats, weights, tackle bits and pieces and spare hooklinks in the pocket of a fly fishing waistcoat, with a bait pouch around my neck. I use two landing nets. For stalking in the jungles I use a 30" round, deep landing net on a short, four feet handle. This might seem a bit small, but it saves getting continuously caught up on brambles and branches. My standard 42" carp landing net serves for all the other mobile stalking sessions.

I think it is the pure simplicity of stalking fish that appeals to me so much. If I can see the bottom and watch as a fish takes the hookbait, I will use either freeline or, at most, light ledger tactics. You have no need for shock rigs and heavy leads. If you're alert at all times you'll know when to strike - it's when the hookbait disappears!

Inevitably you will encounter big carp in among snags at some time or another. I don't want to get too involved with the ethics of snag fishing, other than to say that some very experienced anglers have very serious ethical reservations about snag fishing. Notably the much respected Jim Gibbinson, who has stated his opposition to hook-and-hold fishing and; I must admit, I've seen people fishing some snag situations where I'd rate the chances of extricating a hooked carp at less than 10%, which I feel is totally unacceptable.

However, you can very easily run into a dilemma in your personal assessment of when snag fishing becomes ethically viable. Is it where chances are, say, over 25%, 50%? Where do you draw the line? I guess it's all down to the individual and I'd not want to restrict anyone's right to fish on his own terms. That said, our carp are a precious resource and 'carp at all costs' should not become the popular creed. I'd just hope that nobody would deliberately subject such lovely fish to unnecessary risk.

If you think you've a chance of success, can I suggest the use of float fishing tactics when fishing close to snags? A float will show a take long before a buzzer would make a noise or a monkey begin to climb and the last thing you want is to incite a bolting reaction with modern shock rigs. The carp will be in the snags before you can even blink, let alone pick up the rod. Float techniques allow for that split second advance warning of a pick-up, and you can use this advantage to put the pressure on right from the start, before the hooked fish has time to get any speed up.

Stalking is the essence of carp **hunting** rather than carp fishing. If you are quiet and patient, most stalked carp can be tempted to feed and probably make a mistake, and it's a method that lends itself so well to short, early morning/ late evening sessions. You are at the lake when the fish are most likely to be feeding, rather than sitting out the interminable hours through obvious non-feeding spells - so often the lot of a long session carper.

I could write a book on stalking fish alone, but I appreciate it's not everyone's cup of tea so I'll move on to other tactical aspects we have to consider.

Now, as I mentioned earlier, I don't want to go too deeply into terminal tackle or the often complicated mechanics of rig tuning, as that will be dealt with in another book in this series. However, there are a few generalisations on rigs and hooklinks worth bearing in mind.

The current thinking on rigs seems to revolve in its entirety around the critical balancing of hookbaits. I feel that in many cases this is now being taken too far, though I accept that there are some waters where this will be necessary. Certainly, if a hookbait is fished in total isolation, I can see the point in having ultra fine tuned hookbaits. There are no free offerings with which cautious fish can compare the hookbait, and the idea is to incite a take through suspicious curiosity. Yes, then you may need a rig that jumps into the back of

Ken with a magnificent Savay fish of 25lb 12oz. Ken spent a great deal of time watching Savoy fish feed on baits.

the carp's mouth at the very lightest suck. I think the opposite applies when the carp are feeding hard on a bait.

I have watched the Savay carp feed on standard boiled baits, and there is none of the imagined tear-arsing about that we may imagine. When cautious fish move over a bed of free offerings, it has been my experience that they start slowly, testing several baits before settling down to confident, steady feeding. Obviously, the more food there is in a swim, the more confident they can become (but bear in mind that there are waters where the carp have now become suspicious of huge carpets of bait). The way I see it, the ideal situation, when faced with this feeding pattern, is to have the hookbaits behaving in the same way as the free offerings, and this doesn't mean drawing attention to the hookbait by artificially making it behave so differently by being so much lighter. Surely the carp must regard these in exactly the same way as they would get suspicious of one that was obviously so much heaver than the free offerings. Do you see what I'm getting at? My aim is to make the hookbaits buoyant yes - but only so as to make them behave in the same way as the freebies.

Of course, terminal tackle doesn't just mean the arrangement of the hook and the hair. It includes the hooklink material as well. I believe most firmly that there should be a logical presentation progression, starting with nylon hooklinks and running through Dacron, dental floss and Silkworm, up to Multistrand. I'd suggest most anglers either whizz through the progression too quickly or, worse, go in at the ultimate from day one. There is no need! Look, if the fish are green as grass, simple nylon bolt rigs will fool them for ages - for much longer than most people think. Only when the take rate drops significantly is it time to switch to alternative hooklink materials. I was very happy with Dacron hooklinks for some 5 years and I still use them in many angling situations. As a rule I have always found Dacron to be more effective as a confidence rig hooklink, by which I mean long traces of three feet or more.

The new braids, such as Silkworm and Merlin from Kryston and Nash's Gamabraid, have certainly made for improved presentation but, again, I stress that these extra fine, soft materials are needed only when the fish show signs of getting a bit too cute, and it takes an awful lot of angling pressure to make them that wary.

I am currently fishing a new water where the carp have never been fished for; nylon hooklinks have been scoring well, in conjunction with a good bait. Lately though, some of the anglers on the lake, using sub-standard baits, annoyed at their lower catch rates, have started using the newer braids in the hope of getting more takes. Luckily their bait will still be the limiting factor, but I fear that enough fish may make mistakes and force the rest of us to jump several stages ahead on the progression scale, to a level that wouldn't normally be needed for several seasons.

Surely, you say, if you're catching on the new braids you should be pleased enough? Yes, but there's a well known argument in carp fishing to the effect that 'everything that works for you will one day start to work against you'. So if you go in at the top of the presentation tree, where is there left to go when they start to wise up on even that? Which, I can assure you, they will.

Not so long ago, the new ultra fine nylons such as Drennan's Double Strength, looked as if they might play a useful part in terminal arrangements. However, they seem to have proved something of a damp squib with their low impact strength and lack of strength. The only way to overcome these drawbacks is to use a power gum shock absorber, which I think makes the whole idea impractical.

The length of the hooklink itself can be critical, especially with some of the more sophisticated anti-eject rigs like the bent hook or the silt rig. However, this part of the whole presentation jigsaw offers no hard and fast rule dictating right and wrong on this matter. You might think that shorter hooklinks lead to less effective presentation, but that need not always be the case. For instance, the sliding silt arrangement shown earlier, incorporates a hooklink of three inches. Any longer would work against the presentation leading to poor hook holds and easier ejection. On the other hand, some of the better confidence set ups depend for their efficiency on longer lengths of three feet or so. If it looks as if you are getting plenty of pick ups, but not hooking many carp, it could well be simply the length of the hooklink that is letting you down.

Put yourself in the carp's place and try to imagine what is going on at the business end. If the carp are ultra wary, it could be that they are feeling for resistance from the bomb. Longer hooklinks would cure this, but your hooking arrangement (the rig itself) might not lend itself to longer lengths. For instance, most of the anti-eject rigs work best on short hooklinks of six inches or so. There is really no simple answer. The successful angler is never totally at ease with any terminal arrangement, for the simple reason that eventually fish will wise up to it. By keeping this fact at the back of his mind, he is trying to stay one jump ahead, adjusting and adapting to suit changing conditions.

I think bait is as important a part of the presentation aspect as hooklink or end rig. There is no doubt in my mind that proper, nutritional baits are far more likely to incite confident feeding patterns than poor quality ones, and I've stressed before that I believe complicated terminal rigs lose much of their significance when carp are feeding hard on a good bait.

While we are dealing briefly with the overall importance of bait, I'd like to offer some thoughts on bait preparation. I know it's standard practice to roll baits out these days using Kingfisher Sausage Guns, Gardner Rollaballs or Sidewinders and many weird and wonderful devices that take the hard work out of bait making. I use Gardner bait making gear a hell of a lot, but not always. Sometimes the uniformity of your bait can work against efficient overall presentation.

There are a few little wrinkles to help get around this problem, but before resorting to them, it is worth simply altering the size of your bait. For instance, if the trend on the water is for, say, 15-18mm baits, try the same base made as mini boilies, or go to the other end of the scale with jumbo baits. This simple change of boilie size often gets the carp temporarily confused enough to start falling for the bait again and is the first step change to make when action slows down a bit. Incidentally, don't think that just because takes are getting fewer and farther between, that the bait has necessarily blown. I honestly believe that it takes a lot more pressure than we think to actually blow a bait right out. A heavy baiting campaign, using three or four times as much bait as would normally be used, often re-establishes a bait.

However, when the fishing gets tough, one useful trick is to make a bait mix up in many different sizes and vary the boiling time from 30 seconds up to two minutes. Thus a batch of, say, 400 baits would have several different densities, sizes and degrees of hardness. The varied boiling times affects attractor strength and density with the result that the fish has to treat each bait differently. Differing amounts of suck would be required to hoover up the various sizes. The same applies to 'chew' pressure. Some baits are so soft they almost melted in the carp's lips, others were like rock. I can tell you, they find it very hard to isolate the hookbait then.

One final part of the presentation puzzle is the elimination of tangles. The popular thinking not long ago was, of course, to use anti-tangle tubing. Of late this has largely lost favour, due to the introduction of the helicopter type set-ups and other bomb-on-the-end-of-the-line rigs. However, I think there is much confused thinking about tubing. I'm sure it takes one hell of a lot of individual captures to influence carp and make them spooky of tubing to the extent where they will avoid baits in close proximity to it. I therefore have no qualms about using tubing if required. However, I now mostly use the modern tactic to eliminate tangles, which involves the use of the new Kryston No-Tangle and Super-Stiff Gels for use on Multistrand and braids respectively. Treating the hooklink with this dissolvable gel stiffens them up so that they behave just like the stiff nylon rigs of the past, which seldom tangled. In the water, the gel dissolves and leaves the hooklink in its original limp state.

Finally, the use of stringers will go a long way to eliminating tangles. Always feather the cast down as it nears the water. This allows the bait/stringer to fly ahead of the lead and also reduces the chance of tangles. Remember, not all stringers need to be one straight line of baits tied to the hook bend. The picture on page 79 shows a right mouthful of a set-up that produced fish when the ordinary stringer presentations failed.

Groundbaiting plays an important part in tactical thinking. A lot of anglers think no further on the subject than to fire out willy-nilly a quantity of free offerings into the wide blue yonder: correct groundbaiting tactics will pay dividends so it's worth taking it a bit more seriously than that.

In the section on small waters, I showed how the use of small clumps of PVA tied baits brought success, in conjunction with a hookbait similarly disguised with a clump stringer. I had adapted this trick from one we learnt at Waveney one year when the fish were only making mistakes on double hookbaits. It seemed as if the fish were reacting very cautiously to single hookbaits, and the guys who were taking the fish were not only using double hookbaits, but also taking the trouble to tie up double free offerings as well. You can imagine how this would quickly get under the carp's guard can't you? If all the other double baits lying around can be hoovered up without any problems, surely this one is no different? Here goes - one big suck, both baits at once. Oh no! That's another fine mess you've gotten yourself into!

The amount of free offerings introduced as groundbait needs a good deal of thought these days. Though the standard tactic of bunging in a couple of mixes before fishing and topping up the groundbait with fifty baits per take will still catch fish on most waters, there are some where that approach is the kiss of death. The original thinking behind the 'fill it in' approach was either to get carp used to eating an unnatural foodstuff or to prebait to try and achieve a degree of preoccupation on a bait. These days, most carp need no telling what a boilie is - they see them all the time and know that they represent food – and danger. So much so that there may be times when carp are actually repelled by massive carpets of bait.

I think this might be due to the detection of a large area of the lake bed which has become saturated with the bait's flavour. Remember that most flavours act as primary attractors first and foremost; they tell the fish 'here is food'. They don't force them to eat it. It is one thing to attract carp, clearly another to get them eating your bait. The less pressured they are, the easier this becomes, but the cute fish have long since realised that no matter how attractive the free offerings may be, they spell danger and may well be best ignored. This is where a lighter carpet of groundbait, or even no free offerings at all, may help put a fish on the bank. Certainly, single hookbaits have led to the downfall of many of the country's better known big carp.

Seasonal variations need to be considered when deciding on the amount of groundbait to introduce. It would seem likely that carp are prepared to eat more bait during the summer months than in the depths of winter, but they can really reach their consumption peak during the autumn months of October and November. Their two natural time clocks of falling water temperatures and shorter days tell the carp that winter is near and that they will need to feed hard to build up a cold weather store of fat and condition. At the same time they are also on the lookout for higher protein levels, and I always increase the amount of milk proteins in my bait as winter approaches.

The depths of winter are a different story. In truly cold weather, with water temperatures down below 40 degrees, the fish may not feed for days on end. This is particularly noticeable in settled high pressure conditions. Nevertheless, there may be days when conditions are conducive to heavy and prolonged feeding, and while I usually cut the amount of bait I take for a trip by half in winter, I have, on occasions, been caught out and run out of bait! Only recently, in January 1991, during a bitterly cold spell of easterly weather, I found myself running short of bait after just one day. Six hundred baits went in the first twelve hours, leaving me with just one mix for the remaining thirty six. Needless to say I had five takes in the first day and only one the next. Not enough bait to hold them you see.

There is another groundbaiting technique to look at before we go on. Namely the use of mass baits such as groats, dari seed or hemp seed. Maggots are perhaps one of the very best mass baits, especially in winter, but they can cause problems on mixed fisheries. However, on carp only waters, they are probably the best mass bait of them all. I have noticed a tendency for the fish to get wise to carpets of maggots quite quickly, but before this happens you can really have some bumper catches on the little live baits.

A very high degree of preoccupation can be achieved with these tiny baits, but there are times when this becomes so acute that the carp simply won't look at anything else. I find that contrary to general opinion best results come from fairly light groundbait carpets, rather than the popular trend of filling the swim in with the mass baits. I think the smaller quantity makes the carp more active in searching out the scattering of baits and they don't appear to get so single minded about what they will, or will not, eat.

One sign that things might not all be hunky-dory at the terminal tackle, is single bleeps from the buzzer, rod top knocks or, worse still, just slight line lifts with no other visible or audible indication that the bait has been picked up. Certainly, some of the more aware carp have become adept at picking up hookbaits without necessarily running off in panic and, on some of the pressured waters, the traditional screaming run is becoming something of a rarity. Apart from adjustments to terminal tackle, there are other ways to overcome this situation.

Perhaps the first change should be to switch to heavier bobbins, in conjunction with bankside set ups with the rod tips pointing high in the air. More of the line is visible and any tightening more plainly seen. It also means that the rod tip has now become part of the indication system, as even tiny knocks at the tip will be clearly seen, usually accompanied by a series of single bleeps from the buzzer. (As we've discussed in the tackle section, antenna buzzers have an advantage in these situations as they will buzz continuously as long as an increase in pressure is maintained on the line, but their disadvantage is that they do not show drop back takes).

Switching to heavy bobbins usually means that the number of drop back takes increases. You may also wish to improve sensitivity by installing a twelve vaned beam breaker in your Optonic. Kevin Nash makes these, and for those very cautious fish, they can make all the difference. However, sometimes they can be more trouble than they are worth, and I prefer the ordinary four blade paddle myself.

In the days of the Carp Catchers' Club, the last thing they wanted was any sort of resistance that could be felt by a taking fish. Nowadays, with the advent of the bare hook rigs, we go out of our way to create it. Heavy leads and bobbins make the new rigs work more efficiently, rather than less, but there are times when this resistance works against us when confronted with shy feeding fish. A carp that doesn't move off when it feels the lead and/or hook will not register a take at your end of the tackle. Under these circumstances it is well worth borrowing some ideas from the match fishing fraternity.

It beats me why carp anglers don't make more use of swing and quiver tips. These sensitive bite indicators will show pick ups that wouldn't even register on a bobbin, and certainly wouldn't activate an Optonic - even with a twelve bladed beam breaker. I think the matchman's tactic of aligning the rods parallel to the bank, rather that at right angles, should be given a try, especially with quiver tips. Watch the tip and the line for the slightest movement and strike at it without delay. We know fish on some hard fished waters have now become adept at getting rid of light hook holds, so it's not worth holding on to see if a run develops. Hit it straight away. The same goes for swing tip indications. I think there are many captures waiting to be made on light ledger? swing tip set-ups, perhaps going back to paste baits on the hook and a long paternostered confidence rig.

Finally, just a quick word about the so-called Death Rigs. These are ones that do not allow the lead to be got rid of by the carp in the event of a break off in snags or weed, or a snap off during casting. The one-time habit of attaching the lead direct to the hooklink swivel by means of a snap link is one such rig. The lead is now directly attached to the hooklink and if the fish snaps you up it will be towing the lead around, causing distress, damage and possibly death. There are any number of ways to overcome this and Julian Cundiff's piece on fixed lead fishing in the Carp Society's magazine, Carp Fisher No. 13, spells out most of them. The one rig that hasn't been addressed is the Helicopter. As drawn and used by many anglers, this too is a death rig where it is used in conjunction with a shock or snag leader, or with a 2-3 foot length of sea fishing nylon at the end of the reel line, replacing the tubing and beefing up the stress bearing part of the rig during a fight. The upper bead doesn't go over the shock leader/sea line knot, turning the whole thing into a death rig.

The way to overcome this is to use a rubber shock bead as the upper one. If a break off occurs and the lead gets hung up in snags or weed, the rubber bead will pull over stop knots and joining knots, allowing the fish to swim free with just the hooklink left in its mouth which, hopefully, it will be able to get rid of. Of course, you must ensure that the swivel, ring or bead at the opposite end of the hooklink to the hook itself, is also large enough to pass over the knots etc.

Well, that's all I've got room for. Maybe I've left out some aspect that you think should have been covered, but if I have, I'm sorry. The editor's original remit allowed for a total of 20,000 words to cover both tackle and tactics, and I see I've used all that up on tactics alone!

I hope this little book has helped many of you a new insight to our wonderful sport, by showing some of the nuts and bolts of carp fishing that must be confronted before we even start fishing. It's not all up-front rigs and high-tech baits.

Well worth the waiting. I hope I never tire of it.

Even when you have got it all right there are times when carp fishing can hurt. As Ritchie MacDonald said, "There are times when you just have to sit and wait". That waiting can be the hardest part, but eventually the buzzers scream, the rod bucks and the fight is on. I think it is the anticipation itself that actually **makes** carp fishing for me. I hope I never tire of it.